MONARCHY

To
Victoria, Alexandra, Charlie,
George & Elizabeth

Contents

Future Times

List of Illustrations

Acknowledgements

T o thank those who helped in higher places is an inadequate expression, but it'll have to do. Those who advised and suggested and who inhabit grand (yet often shabby) corridors did not want names mentioned. I am not sure why that should be. Be it is, so I shall respect that. The use of the Ipsos-Mori polling was invaluable even though it is all in the public domain. Pulling it together in this way puts monarch and monarchy in distinct perspective. Anthony Weldon, whose ancestor was so close to monarchy in an apparently satisfying manner (at least for the then monarch herself who borrowed a sword to ceremonially bless him), has been encouraging in nudging through the idea during never overly-long luncheons in St James and patient when a deadline was missed—on one occasion when I had to down tools to comment at the BBC on the funeral and its arrangements for the late Baroness Thatcher. Then of course there has to be a sure indication of my ever appreciation of the way staff in the Music and Rare Books Reading Room at the British Library continue to be the best friends a sometimes muddle-morning writer can have. The opinions, interpretations and conclusion, of course, are all mine.

Introduction

The twenty-first-century British monarchy is unambiguously aligned to concepts of Saxon kingship and the Christian Church, and the influence of both continue to be inconclusively debated. Moreover, as with many other monarchies, the British crown is since the eighteenth century dynastical. Thus the modern monarch is linked to the history of a millennium of British crowns, even though the families are not necessarily so. It is our purpose neither to record a history of kings and queens of England nor to judge each as a 'good thing/king' or otherwise. Therefore, what follows is the painting of an impression of the march of monarchy after the Normans' invasion and, in making it, the development of a notion of why, say, the British and Japanese monarchies have lasted so long.

In earlier centuries, island nations have been harder to conquer. Tides, weather conditions, limitations of boat construction and stability, and thus restrictions on reinforcements and logistics, suggest island monarchies have been simpler to defend or, put another way, harder to attack. Even during the later Middle Ages and Tudor centuries, when the English were threatened with invasion by the exceptionally ambitious—and papally encouraged—Catholic French and Iberian monarchies, the advantage was always with the islanders. The most quoted example has been the planned invasion by the Spanish in 1588.

MONARCHY

The Armada was dispersed by terrible weather conditions. Even if it had landed, the Spanish and mercenary force would have faced formidable resistance from conditions ashore.

More than two centuries later, Napoleon's extraordinarily ambitious plans (at least fourteen of them) to invade from Boulogne were partially thwarted by his seemingly total lack of understanding of the limitations of larger vessels, tidal conditions, hull designs and beach reconnaissance.[1] However, the fact that the British Isles were hard to penetrate does not entirely explain the survival of the monarchy. Duke William invaded successfully, but the British monarchy did not fall. Only the Saxon house of Godwine was overcome. The Danish monarchy as a throne that ruled the state as well as the people began in the first half of the tenth century and the first sovereign was Gorm the Old.

In theory, the Danish monarch was elected, although the crown without exception was successfully claimed by the eldest son in line and in 1660 (the date, coincidentally, of the re-establishment of the English monarchy) the constitutional elective monarchy was dropped in favour of an hereditary manner of succession. Four years later, this was reinforced to honour primogeniture so that the male line was guaranteed. It was not until 1953 that an Act of Succession made way for a queen. There were no outside pressures for these changes. Just as constitutional affectations came from within the British system, so they did in other monarchies. The illustration of the Danish royal line becomes significant when we consider one of the most important themes in the monarchy of quite different nations—the gradual thought that many and sometimes, at different periods in the history of state monarchy, all monarchies were related, and remain so.

Long before Britain had a king who ruled the land mass as well its peoples it was not unusual for a victorious chieftain, and so later a king, to signal the end of the conflict, even a battle, by marrying one of his children either to the defeated or victorious opposing king, or to one of his children. In effect, the joining of the two families was the most uncomplicated sign of peace. For hundreds of years before even Hastings, we have good evidence of post-war arranged weddings between former

[1] See Lee, Christopher, *Nelson and Napoleon*, Headline, London, 2005.

enemies. Many of them would continue to be enemies, but the symbolism was clear: the Saxon king would give a daughter to the invading monarch. For example, one of King Alfred's daughters, Aetheflaed, was given in marriage to the Ealdorman of Mercia (and later became Mercia's queen) and another, Aelfthryth, was married off to the Count of Flanders. Without relying on brides as war trophies, more recent European royal families also interwed; in Denmark's case, King Christian IX was the father-in-law of Europe. His first daughter, Princess Alexandra, married Queen Victoria's heir Bertie, the then Prince of Wales, and so became Queen Alexandra. Another of Christian IX's princesses, Dagmar, married Tsar Alexander III of Russia; Princess Thyra (1853–1933) married the Crown Prince of Hanover and the Third Duke of Cumberland and Teviotdale, Ernst August (1845–1923), who was a second cousin of the future Edward VII. It was his son, William, or Wilhelm, who in 1863 became King of the Hellenes (Greece) as George I. Here was the line from which the husband of Elizabeth II, Prince Philip, descended. The very erratic nature of the claims and counterclaims on European territories and thrones during the Middle Ages emphasised dynastic identities of what we would now see as complete states or countries, whereas, say, five or six centuries ago, the sovereignty of peoples did not assure sovereignty of state. Thus once more we find intermarriage by desire or convenience (mostly the latter), and therefore later claim and counterclaim on authority of regions and greater states.

The Spanish throne has a broken hereditary line, but the present monarchy dates from the eighth century and only the Japanese monarchy is older. Above all, Spain is a simple example of earlier societies undergoing similar transitions quite independently of each other, but with not dissimilar effects. The Vikings invaded the British Isles from across the sea in similar manner to the Arab invasion of the Iberian Peninsula during the seventh and the eighth centuries. Just as Britons withdrew into regional strongholds before the Danish advances, so the Arabs—the Moors—had the Christian Iberians, with their royal Visigothic origins in the fifth century, on the run into the northern regions. Although the eleventh-century King of Navarre, Sancho III, is credited with beginning the fight-back to reclaim Iberia, it took some four centuries before the Moors were defeated and Spain became three regions, Navarre, Aragon and Castile. Again, what we saw in Saxon

England—the marriage of a royal daughter to a sometime enemy—was a common tactic to unite warring factions and cultural opposites. Just as in England, this did not always work. For example, when in the early 1100s, the King of Aragon married the heiress of Castile, the diplomatic ruse failed because their DNA was too similar and the consequent consanguinity made it impossible to maintain the dynasty.

The textbook union did eventually work when Ferdinand II of Aragon married Isabel of Castile in 1469. Famously, it was Catherine of Aragon, Catalina de Aragón, who, at just three years old, was promised to the heir to the English throne, Prince Arthur, Prince of Wales. They married in 1501 when she was eighteen. But Arthur died inside six months of the marriage and eight years later she was married to her late husband's younger brother, who had acceded as Henry VIII. She followed a style and pattern in linked royalties. Catherine, the daughter of John of Gaunt and granddaughter of King Peter of Castile and Spain until his death in battle in 1369, was married to Castile's Henry III. Their son, John, became King of Castile from 1406 to 1454. The Iberian family of nobles was endorsed when John II then married a second wife (his first, Maria of Aragon, gave him four children), Isabella of Portugal.

This brief wiring diagram of Iberian royalty is expected to do little more than show why it is impossible to imagine that the linked history of continental European royal and lower noble houses may not be seen in isolation; royalty ruled well beyond its own borders. The greatest regal influence in Europe was the Austrian Habsburg dynasty, originating in the ninth century and led by elected Holy Roman Emperors from the early fifteenth to the eighteenth centuries. Through the family Habsburg lines, claim could be made to either direct ruling titles or consort titles in Aragon, Bohemia, Castile, Croatia, Dalmatia, England and Ireland, Galicia, Germany, Hungary, Naples, Portugal, Sicily, Spain and the Archdukedom of Austria.

This is worth remembering when we follow the trails left by royalty and thus the monarchy of almost one thousand years since Hastings. The broad dynastical categories are useful because they easily match the moods and consequences of the times that are popularised by even faintly recognisable images, and because of the obvious extension that kings and queens do not have many different names. Edward is the longest surviving royal name. Since the invasion there have been few different royal first names: Edward (eight), Henry (eight), George (six), William (four), Richard (three), Elizabeth (two), Mary (two), Anne (one), Victoria (one). Moreover, there have been just seven British royal houses since 1066: Normandy, Anjou (Henry II, Richard I and John were Angevins), Plantagenet, Tudor, Stuart, Hanover and Windsor. Starting with William of Normandy (William I of England) in the aftermath of 1066, what of the sixty British monarchs (forty-one English and nineteen Scottish[2]) since that moment at Hastings and why might we (or might we not) remember them? One obvious 'what of?' is the fact that, following the Saxon kings, the English monarchs and many of the Scottish kings stayed on the throne for a goodly period. More importantly, what was the contribution to the lot of the people of these islands and, in the case of the post-Tudors, to the lot of what would become a quarter of the globe? Until the emergence of structured parliamentary government it was certainly the monarch who influenced the way people lived within a society increasingly legislated for.

Queen Anne in the eighteenth century was the last British monarch to veto parliamentary legislation, although given the sense of military rebellion over Anglo-Scottish Union passed the previous year, 1707, the queen was not being as autocratic as some may believe, never mind the fact that she had just been through a constitutional confrontation with her government; she had been forced to sack the Speaker, Robert Harley, and her Catholic half-brother, James Stuart, had only just failed to land in Scotland to lead an uprising against the English.[3] The purpose here is to illustrate that, at a time in the seventeenth century of the development of party-political government, the monarch had considerable political power. That power survived into the eighteenth century and only slowly declined over the following eight or nine decades. Even Edward VII exercised political influence, if not direct power.

The British have had a monarchy that has had a considerable say in the ways of the country until just a hundred years ago. When it has been forced to back down, even in the face of overwhelming challenges

---

[2] See page 183.
[3] In 1708 Queen Anne refused to sign a Bill to restructure the Scottish Militia and introduce it into Scotland. Her objection was supported by her ministers because since the Bill had been passed there was a fear that the militia would not be loyal.

from the magnates and barons, the monarchy has regrouped and survived. Its very public position has meant that it has differed from the governing aristocracy in one particular aspect: by and large, the monarch has always been for the people; the barons have not been. Thus the monarchy may on occasions have astounded the constitutional protocols of its very existence, but it has survived thus far. Moreover, in most reigns the individual monarch of the time has outlasted the aristocracy and class that would govern the people. To judge the historical value of the monarchy during the times since 14 October 1066, we might spend a little time looking at what was as well as what was not achieved by the men and women who ruled in truth and those who did so with more modest powers.

The British have a global identity inasmuch as they live in a place that has known history, largely through images of monarchs and deeds of empire. It is a generous but understandable image, because British society past and present has an internationally recognised constant: for more than a thousand years the people of the British Isles have been ruled by kings and queens. First the king ruled by the sword and the reward of kingship. Then came the uncertainty of constitutional monarchy. Finally, as it is now, the monarchy was simply there; harmless, hardly divisive, and even perhaps loved as an institution and loved in the manner a population might do so because the monarch is the identity of the nation.

Thinking, therefore, about the future of the British monarchy means more than asking whether or not it is time for it to go and, if it did go, whether it should be replaced, and with what. That would suggest the debate is between royalist and republican; both have leading voices in any discussion, but the thought must explore the future and not the conclusion or otherwise of the longest lived institution that has dominated British identity for more than ten centuries. If the British monarchy survives the twenty-first century, what will it look like? In that time frame, by how much might the identity of the British change and what might be the cause of that change? For change there will surely be and with it will come the alterations, even disappearances, of the increasingly vulnerable bone-structures of any society, the institutions. Monarchy is by far the longest lived of them.

The immediate thought must be about the likelihood of a national debate and the circumstances causing the debate. It would take only a senior royal death to prompt discussion among the British people and the governments of more than fifty other states about the future of the monarchy. The English-speaking peoples and British colonial history, together with the international image of wealth, position and more than a thousand-year history of royal figures, from the mythical King Arthur to the very real and documented Diana, Princess of Wales, have created an internationally unsurpassed theatre of grandeur, privilege, admiration and, above all, the promise of protection in return for loyalty. Moreover, with few and exceptional glitches in the apparently universal popularity of Elizabeth II, successive opinion polls have shown throughout much of the British Isles a consistent support for the monarch, with variations appearing in support for the institution of monarchy. The Queen has reigned above any questions of whether it is right or wrong that the United Kingdom in the twenty-first century should politically and socially support one of the most privileged families anywhere in the world.

The Queen's primary role during more than sixty years has been to protect the system of constitutional monarchy. Opinion polling suggests she has succeeded. The next stage in the British monarchy may not be so sure-footed. That is not stated as some tabloid cliché to excite debate. It is a fact of an advancing and changing society at a pace never before recorded. Moreover, Queen Elizabeth II has richly shown the distinction of monarchy and incumbent. Certainly in 2012, the year of her Diamond Jubilee, there was little evidence that the general public thought her heir Charles, Prince of Wales, would be a popular successor. There was even talk in the British media and, therefore, presumably among her people, that the succession should skip a generation, so that the Duke of Cambridge, Prince William, should become king on the death of his grandmother. This idea was constitutionally unacceptable yet there was nothing to stop parliamentary drafting and approval for a law that would make it possible if monarch and government thought it best.

There is every indication that the Queen was little surprised at this concept. For more than a decade, she could not have been anything else but aware of the changing relationship between royal family and British people. A twelve-month period two decades earlier had been described by the Queen herself as her *'annus horribilis'*. Nineteen-ninety-two was the year in which the Prince of Wales and Diana separated. It was the year in which Diana, through the pages of Andrew Morton's biography, *Diana: Her True Story*, laid out what the public had long believed: that her marriage had been a sham, that she had lovers and that the royal family had to a severe degree done little or nothing to help the marriage survive.

It was the same year that the consistently most popular of the Queen's children, Princess Anne, was divorced from Captain Mark Phillips, and as if more was always to come, photographs appeared in newspapers and magazines of a topless Sarah, the estranged wife of the Queen's third child, Prince Andrew, Duke of York, having her toes sucked by her financial adviser. There was yet more: tapes of an astonishingly intimate and indiscreet telephone conversation between Prince Charles and the then Mrs Camilla Parker Bowles, dubbed by tabloids as 'Camillagate', and then another personal telephone conversation between Diana and one of her lovers, James Gilbey, similarly named 'Squidgygate'.

If there is a case that the monarch reflects the identity of his or her people, the dysfunctional image of the royal family reflected the growing trend in the United Kingdom of marriages and personal relations failing, with little effort, to hold them together. It took a tragedy for the Windsors, steered by the Queen, to put their public image into some sort of order. 'Image' is not the wrong word; the royal family had long ceased to be truly royal. By the Diana period they were reduced to a house of celebrities. The tragedy for reform came in August 1997 with the news that the most famous of the family had been killed in a Paris underpass.

After the death of Diana, it was clear that there had been a shift in public perception of the royal family and the monarchy. Thus it was the confusing of royalty and celebrity, and not constitutional politics and opinion, that brought about change. While there was no question of a republican tendency, the monarchy was vulnerable to reform and therefore it had best reform itself. From this came a series of regular meetings of officials and members of the royal family known as the Way Ahead Group. The royal family was not always in agreement on these occasions. The underlying feeling was so often that the Way Ahead Group was implicitly talking about more than style; it was discussing the very future of the British monarchy.

More than that, the strong debate included the extended royal family. Few doubted the role of the Queen and her sense of duty. Many doubted the value to the nation of the immediate family, especially Prince Edward and Prince Andrew, suggesting that the role of the further royals is harder to support. What next? Within a decade the future of the monarchy will be influenced by very public events:

- First, the Duke and Duchess of Cambridge's son has prompted the question: will he be king one day?
- Second, the Camelot of William and Catherine will encourage the discussion that the succession should jump a generation. Charles and Camilla are taking on more duties, but their public image that rallied during and after the 2012 Jubilee is, a year on, losing ground to the Cambridges. Age will not weary the accession of the Prince of Wales and the Duchess of Cornwall, but it will give energy to the debate. Generation-jumping is not constitutionally possible unless there is an impediment in the line, and in that case the road would lead to a regency.
- Third, the Queen at eighty-seven looks well, but vulnerable. She may not rely on Sister Agnes[4] to hold on to her. Her personal constitution may be enviable, but the constitution of her realm is about to go under the political knife.
- Fourth, the debate over the future of the House of Lords and the revision of the 1701 Act of Settlement will need to be decided, at least in some principle, by 2015. It is a hard constitutional path to tread, for it will lead to the bigger question: for how long does the United Kingdom remain a monarchy and in what form should the monarchy exist during its remaining years? England has had a monarch since the tenth century, but along with the authority of all institutions in the United Kingdom, royalty is in decline. Does this mean the monarchy's end is in sight?

---

[4] King Edward VII's Hospital, London, founded in 1899 and named Sister Agnes, after a very close friend of the then Prince of Wales, Agnes Keyser, who started the hospital in her Belgravia home.

- Fifth, the Church of England will be disestablished and with it the role of the monarch as supreme governor—the last duty of the monarch that gives authority to a state church, particularly over Roman Catholicism.
- Sixth, no one can be sure of the consequences of Scottish independence.

If replacement occurs, what options follow? There is little sign of republicanism on a large scale in the United Kingdom. The phrase 'usual suspects' would be appropriate. The British seem unlikely to take to the streets in protest against the monarch, or the monarchy. Yet public opposition is not necessarily a force that will bring down royalty in the United Kingdom. Far more likely is the break-up of the united kingdoms of Northern Ireland, Scotland, Wales and England.

The process of devolved government to whatever level of authority was a weakening of the identity of the United Kingdom and this identity reflected in the monarchy was thus defaced. Moreover, when government wonders aloud about multiculturalism, British society is likely to be thinking about changing public influences in the British Isles. It is then that all institutions, including the monarchy, come face to face with incisive scrutiny not experienced before. Assessing public feeling towards changing values in institutions and public perceptions of those values is not as easy as may be imagined. Opinion polls and focus groups may be uncannily consistent, but they too are vulnerable to public fickleness and even a mass instinct to give the answer they think the interrogator wishes to hear.

One of the more reliable recent poll results (YouGov) suggests that on balance the country supports the monarchy. However, within those figures, there are signs that attitudes would change after the Queen's death. For example, only thirty per cent think that Prince Charles should become head of the established Church—a significant role for the monarch, as successive kings and queens since George III and Catholic emancipation have insisted. A Charles monarchy courts debate that teeters on controversy. As another example, only eight per cent think he and the Duchess of Cornwall would be popular as king and queen. Ignoring the history of the Hanoverians and in particular the reputations of successive Princes of Wales, just fourteen per cent of those polled believe that the monarchy sets a good example to the rest of society. Again, given public contempt for many once trusted institutions, the monarchy is looked on as one part of society to maintain standards. Your standards are old-fashioned, Mr Bennett. Yes, madam, replied the great man, that's why they are standards. Public polling suggests that the present monarch would understand Mr Bennett's reply, but her successors might not.

An averaging of recent polling suggests that the monarchy is included in institutions that have lost some of the trust of the general public and are in fact below other institutions. The following may help to illustrate this point—starting with the good news for the monarchy.

Younger people, generally accepted as the nineteen-to-thirty age range, appear to think that on balance the monarchy is fine, but would have more chance of surviving if it skipped a generation. There is a general ignorance of the constitutional process that says that this is unlikely other than in the form of a regency and all that that would mean. Moreover, polling supports this generation-jumping view among middle-class and middle-age groupings. Prince William's marriage strengthened this opinion.

A new royal baby means another generation in waiting and that there is a further claim on the succession. The question then is: does the evidence of changing societies within the United Kingdom suggest that the firstborn of the Cambridges will not become monarch, because there will be no monarchy?

Times Past

CHAPTER ONE

The First Kings of England

There are some 192 countries in the world. More than forty of them have monarchs.[1] Of them all, Japan has the oldest uninterrupted monarchy and its present dynasty is traced in an unbroken line to the fifth century AD and the beginnings of the Yamato state. In Europe, the Danish monarchy was established in the tenth century, as was the British monarchy, although the execution of King Charles I in 1649 interrupted for eleven years the dynastical rule of the British. However,

---

[1] Bahrain, Belgium, Bhutan, Brunei, Cambodia, Denmark, Japan, Jordan, Kuwait, Lesotho, Liechtenstein, Luxembourg, Malaysia, Monaco, Morocco, the Netherlands, Norway, Oman, Qatar, Saudi Arabia, Spain, Swaziland, Sweden, Thailand, Tonga, the United Kingdom and sixteen other members of the Commonwealth with the British monarch as head of state: Australia, Antigua and Barbuda, the Bahamas, Barbados, Belize, Canada, Grenada, Jamaica, New Zealand, Papua New Guinea, Saint Kitts and Nevis, the Solomon Islands, Tuvalu, Saint Lucia, Saint Vincent and the Grenadines. There are, too, the collection of British overseas territories that have the monarch as head of state: Anguilla, Bermuda, British Indian Ocean Territory, the British Virgin Islands, the Cayman Islands, the Falkland Islands, Gibraltar, Montserrat (BOT), the Pitcairn Islands, Saint Helena, Ascension and Tristan da Cunha, South Georgia and the South Sandwich Islands, and the Turks and Caicos Islands. Thus the sun may have long set over the British Empire, but not over the territories where the British monarch reigns.

given that the next king was in exile during the Commonwealth, in theory the British monarchy has an unbroken line since the tenth century and so is the second longest in the world.

There have been fifty-three sovereigns of England since the tenth century.[2] Yet in spite of the frailties and even failures of the individuals, only one, Charles I, angered the system and its magnates enough to be executed, and a decade later the monarchy was restored. This constitutional institution has been the least divisive aspect of the British people for a thousand years. That should be enough argument to insist there is no case for the disappearance of the monarchy, but it is not. Society and its ambitions are changing faster than the institution of monarchy. Very simply, monarchy could become irrelevant, gradually noticed as such and then vulnerable to personality shifting into another form.

To reflect the significance of monarchy and identity in the twenty-first century, it is not enough to take the existing monarch and set it up as the image and characteristics of that sovereign's people or, more explicitly, the form of modern monarchy and the profile drawn from that matrix. To understand monarchy and its origins at times we deal with an uneasy symbolism in a society given a general and certainly generic term, 'British'. In doing so, it is best to explore how that monarchy arrived as ruler, not simply of the people in a tribal sense, but of the considerably more powerful version, the ruler of a state which those people recognised as their original home. Nothing may be taken for granted. The origin of kings and peoples is not as well understood as might be expected.

Few events other than the Saxon defeat at the Battle of Hastings, the excitement of Tudor England and the origins of the Second World War are important in school history lessons. Little of the kings, other than the mythical Arthur and the cake-burning (or most likely not) Alfred, is taught. The first English historian, Bede, is rarely studied or even read; the prose is testing and the variations are too complex to skip from one to the other, and even at secondary level teachers avoid it. It could be of course that the primary source is set aside because Saxon history is left to its monuments—small, interesting churches, but rarely visited—and the mythology of people and places too difficult

---

[2] Lady Jane Grey was proclaimed queen, but did not succeed.

for a less and less inquisitive twenty-first-century English society. That Westminster Abbey was the inspiration of a Saxon king and that Emma of Normandy was, in modern style if we wish, game-changer and Saxon play-maker can excite little interest other than the bald fact; little more is truly known of Emma anyway. Even the Normans struggle to get further than pictorial essays in the historically important era when the Pembrokeshire descendants of the Conqueror's knights were the mercenary defenders and then the stock of Irish aristocracy.

Surprisingly today, with ranging media histories, few would know that the Tower of London is of Norman origin, or that Domesday had an administrative purpose, or that the Normans became Angevins became Plantagenets; the last Plantagenet—if remembered outside Shakespeare's version—was Richard III. To be discovered beneath a Leicester car park is hardly a memorial to someone who is said to have caused the deaths of the Princes in the Tower; but in a snapshot survey for this writing, not a single person of 168 questioned knew the names of the princes and most certainly not their dates.[3]

The English have seemingly believed that the territory of England was populated by the English. The Welsh have felt the same about themselves. Such an obvious statement should not be dismissed when understanding monarchy because, for example, opinion suggests that the inhabitants of Scotland have not always believed that the land was occupied by people essentially Scottish. When claims were made on who should rule even parts of Scotland, never mind the whole territory, the right to be monarch of more than one glen was not so straightforward.

The establishment of a monarch of Scotland and England, and to a lesser extent Wales, tells the British the first thing they should know of their heritage: the point at which their country became a free-standing state. For the monarch was not simply leader of the people. He or later she was head of state, and thus the state and the beginnings of national identity were recognised by outsiders. The immediate outsiders were the peoples abutting the declared state and so, as an example, Scotland

---

[3] If the sons of Edward IV, twelve-year-old Edward V of England and his brother, nine-year-old Richard, Duke of York, were murdered, it would have happened in 1483, the year Edward V was to have been crowned. What may have been their remains were uncovered in 1674 and reburied in Westminster Abbey by order of Charles II.

had to accept England as a state, or suffer the seemingly continuous penalty of incursion, intervention and, ultimately, war. Here, then, is part of the origins of national identity.

To be sure-footed in this search for the relationship between monarchy and peoples, we have to piece together the wiring diagrams of English, Welsh and Scottish monarchies until we can reach a point when we reasonably accept that the monarch was leader of the state as well as the people, even if that latter distinction were to be contested in civil war. It tells us more about our inherited instincts than we might normally imagine exist.

Therefore, what follows is not a biographical note on kings and queens. It is the story of how royalty was established in England, Wales and Scotland by the Middle Ages, and so it will explain causes that established the authority of monarchy that exist in those three territories, even before they were countries, and among those three peoples. Here was regional, tribal and family leadership. If that would appear obvious, then it is a statement to show that in small lands, such as those in the British islands, monarchy and principality were established along with the fundamental need for people to be brought together to protect the interests of the most powerful. It was to protect basic kingship in which a powerful leader promises to protect those never to be powerful in return for an allegiance necessary for the chieftain to safeguard his as well as their interests. In the later form, that same kingship attempted to protect its people from more than a foreign invader. It also had a duty to protect them from government and government's ambitions for some or all the territory.

The first to rule over the territory or state of England, as opposed to just the greater tribe known as the English, was Athelstan, between AD 924 and 939. During the 1,089 years that England, then Britain, then the United Kingdom have been ruled by a sovereign, the extraordinary presence of a persistent system of rule and often unpredictable variation of character has offered a singular and not-to-be-forgotten given: the reigning monarch is not to be confused with monarchy. The king or queen is but the holder of that crowned office. A popular or unpopular monarch necessarily supports or damages the institution, but in neither case is the sole reason for its survival or abolition. Therefore, to understand the future of monarchy, it is first necessary to separate the personality from the institution. We need to understand the history of monarchy, especially in the United Kingdom in whose capital lives the monarch of one-third of those countries that retain a throne.

It is here that we need to grasp the first distinction of monarchy: a monarch may rule people without ruling the greater territory in which they live. For example, Alfred the Great was king of the people of Wessex, but he was never King of England. He did not rule England. In fact, at that time, we cannot even properly say that England existed in a form we would easily recognise today. Other kings and invaders ruled other parts of the islands. To make this important distinction clearer, imagine a mass migration, for whatever reason, from one part of a continent to another: the monarch is still monarch of the people, but he or she is most certainly not monarch of the new territory. The monarchy of a state implies others bordering and beyond that state recognising the authority of the monarch, whereas a monarch of the people only (and it could be that the population is the same size in whatever condition) could be little more than a tribal leader with no rights over the territory, even when his people live in it.

Certainly before the Christian era, there were thousands of years of monarchs, but it is unlikely that until the Japanese dynasties (well after the establishment of the Christian age) there were unbroken, family-associated lines of monarchs, as we would today understand the concept. It is too easy to regard a king or queen in distant times as simply a military leader. To do so would miss one of the important aspects of kingship that continues in part in the twentieth century: the religious, even god-like authority of monarchy. We hear of the divine right of kings. By that simple phrase, we accept that the authority of the monarch is god-given and, in some instances, the monarch is seen as a divine figure. A modern example would be the Japanese emperor who, until shortly after the Second World War, claimed spiritual though not godly significance—more, that he was the conduit to god.

The British monarch is head of the Church of England here on earth and, according to a 2012 opinion poll, this pleases the population.[4]

---

[4] Seventy-three per cent said Elizabeth II should continue as supreme governor of the Church of England and keep the Defender of the Faith title first given to Henry VIII. (Source: ComRes.)

Emperor Hirohito of Japan. In the Shinto religion, he was a descendant
of the Sun-Goddess. After World War II and the nuclear bombing of Japan,
Hirohito announced that he was not a god.

In China, the emperor most certainly had a mystical authority in a society drawn easily to animism—the existence of spirits and souls in earthly communion—long before the structure of a belief in a single and universal god.[5] It may be imagined that a monarch assuming godly distinction would be vulnerable when the good times faltered. Crop failures, terrible weather, famine, disease and of course lost battles were all conditions that called into question a king's heavenly credentials. Waning powers or those fraudulently claimed could easily signal the end of a monarch's reign. In some societies, a monarch might be expected to fall on his sword or drink a final draught as the gossamer of heavenly authority parted. Furthermore, because the priesthood had remarkable responsibility in the choice, crowning and ritual of a monarch, the king would have to recognise the considerable power of the priests over the throne. Consequently, the religious patriarch might assume an authority greater than the monarch.

Whatever authority and however strong or weak that authority on the throne, the monarch was hardly a fairytale, rags-to-riches appointment. The individual who became king was likely, first, to be a powerful individual with considerable physical and political support, and therefore, second, already a member of privileged society and in some parts of the world able to claim family line to the throne. However, primogeniture, the right of inheritance of the first-born child, was not always clear. A society in which it was commonplace for an individual to have more than one wife (or concubine) was vulnerable to dispute over who exactly should inherit, even if this were made comparatively simple by a convention that the first male born would take precedence. This, at the time of writing, is no longer the case. The first born is heir.

The importance of proof of the parenthood of the monarch's proposed heir could never be underrated or, in some cases, guaranteed. Shortening the list of candidates by giving precedence to male heirs did not necessarily rid courts and factions of suspicions that the line of royal succession might be corrupt. There can be few offices of state in any society so vulnerable to corruption than the monarchy. The inspiration of patronage alone makes monarchy an easy target for political,

---

[5] *Anima* (Latin): breath, soul, life, air.

personal and commercial jealousies. Because most in civil ignorance never and could never have truly known the workings of the monarchy in their own country, rumour and gossip are eagerly believed. This increased the need of the monarchy to maintain its credibility, often by creating an imagined crisis, then leading the people to safety as leader, as part-divine monarch of people of similar sect and language and later, as territorial definitions became clearer, dynastical monarch of a nation state and defender of the people in return for their allegiance.

Later, especially in western Europe, came the creation of a constitutional monarchy without any powers that influenced the course of the people, but was necessarily maintained even by republican tendencies. The instincts of the people suggested that contrary to all ideological discipline a monarch, even in titular form, was necessary to reassure them that a system and an individual, no matter how fanciful, represented what they stood for as a nation people. This is the irony of modern monarchy: the unelected leader is closer to the people than the government that the people elected to rule. It follows that monarchy gives a nation state its identity. The default observation of those ruled, as well as those beyond that society, is that the king must be a leader who, on balance, is supported by those who in other circumstances are in a position to usurp the monarch's authority and rule in his place. The people ruled and outside observers have a single view of the monarch: a superior person ruling by a right—even a divine right—to which none of his or her subjects could ever aspire. The further irony is that the monarch is rarely the leader of the nation's aristocracy. Indeed, the monarch may be seen as middle class. Where does the etymology place the origins of the supreme titles in these societies? Whatever the divine beliefs of the incumbent, unlike the concept of kingship, there is rarely anything god-like in these origins.

King comes from the Old English *cyning*, queen from *cwen* (woman). Unusually, 'queen' is not a female title derived from the male word as, for example, 'empress' is from 'emperor'. *Cyning* has within it 'kin', as in family. *Cyning* suggests the ruler of the family or leader of the people. The words 'monarch' and 'monarchy' have an earlier origin. 'Monarch' comes from the Greek *monos*, one, or alone, and *archein*, to rule. In ancient Greece, an *archon* was one of the nine magistrates ordered to rule. We have a monarch as one who rules by him- or herself; it was a term in common British usage by the 1300s. But ruling what? Tribe? People? Land? Supremely, it was a combination of all three that was recognised by outsiders. As early as 55 BC, Cassivellaunus could be described as a king of the Catuvellauni—the people who for so long opposed Julius Caesar in Britain. In AD 43, there was no sterner warrior king than Caractacus, none more famous than Boudicca in AD 61, and the walls and ditches the Romans left behind witness the powers of great warrior kings in these islands. Yet they were kings of tribes, not kings of the English, certainly not the British and most definitely not of England or Britain. A thousand years passed after the successful Roman invasion of Britain before there was a king of England. To imagine that perspective, it is today more or less a thousand years since the Battle of Hastings. But to get a grasp of what monarchy was to mean, we have to go further back in this island history, to the arrival from north continental Europe of the Saxons.

To think, in haste, through the importance of William of Normandy and everything that followed, from Angevin to Plantagenet, there is a tendency to overlook the significance of Saxon England. The Angles, Saxons and Jutes were regular raiders from their settlements in Germany and south Denmark, and began to settle in England, or in the then dominant Gaelic Sasana—hence Sassenachs—in the fifth century. The continental tribes referred to these people as 'Saxons' which, by the eighth century, had picked up the word for English, 'Angli', and so became the 'Anglo-Saxons', the English Saxons. Certainly by the fifth century they controlled England south of the line running from the Wash to the Solent. One consequence of this invasion was the ravaging of the Christian Church. Anglo-Saxons claimed no divine right to rule and the British expected no divine protection. The sixth-century British monk Gildas (c. 500–570) proclaimed in his most famous work, *De excidio et conquestu Britanniae*, that the invasion was God's punishment for the waywardness of the Britons.

Germany had no monarchy, just local chieftains. The Anglo-Saxons might have been seen as tribal leaders without a sense of all-important kingship. Yet this was not such a straightforward conclusion. A tribal leader may not have developed the moral instincts that modern reflections laid upon the subject; equally, a chieftain practised kingship in another name with a similar principle. He would protect his people in return for their loyalty and it should be a logical progression at tribal level for a leader with greater responsibilities—more people and further-flung territory—to develop within Anglo-Saxon England the concept of kingship. The circumstances found in England following the Anglo-Saxon settlement were fertile enough for kingship to take root. Importantly, the Saxons elected their leaders. Those leaders had, in theory, their powers limited by the people, and when we understand the origins of the settlers who came from small and simple communities, we understand more easily that the early Saxons in Britain were very much a people of equals. The gap between rich and poor was narrow, which is perhaps one reason to suspect that although the elected leaders were hardly hamstrung, their powers were not absolute. What broadened the gap between the leaders and their close followers was warfare.

The leaders by their very election were attractive warriors, and bagged much treasure from skirmishes and battles. They took the largest slice of that lucrative plunder. With increased wealth they grew above the foot soldiers and bought the recognition and loyalty of their closest lieutenants, who then had every incentive to keep the leaders in power and in so doing give them even more power. Power stretches from the top to the lieutenants and becomes patronage. There was no more valuable convertible currency than this in Saxon England. All the above built its own authority and gradually the leader had absolute long-term power. 'The power and the permanence coalesced into kingship.'[6] This is the era when tribal Anglo-Saxon leaders in England became regional leaders, and expanded their ambitions and the need to govern more territory—as in the cases of Redwald, Aethelfrith, Aethelbert, Penda, Offa and Egbert. In doing so, there developed the complex agreement between leaders and people of kingship. Yet we return to the warning that kingship did not mean that one man ruled the whole land. Again, for example, leaders such as Alfred the Great were not kings of England. These islands were split into a series of fiefdoms. The kings were never monarchs of all they surveyed, only of the pieces they could defend. Alfred, though credited as founder of the Royal Navy, was only King of Wessex.

A scan of the powerful areas of England and Scotland gives an

[6] Starkey, David, *Crown & Country*, p.24, Harper Press, London, 2011.

Anglo Saxon Kingdoms c.800. It was not until 924 that England was ruled by one monarch.

image of the boundaries (sometimes shifting) of the military and monarchy divisions in the isles: Wessex, Sussex, Kent, Essex, East Anglia, Mercia (Middle England) and Northumbria. Thus, when Essex and Middlesex were proclaimed in about AD 527, they were so as kingdoms and therefore with monarchies. In 597, Augustine (later Saint Augustine) arrived in Kent and founded the Benedictine monastery with the blessing of the by then Christian convert King Aethelbert (sometimes 'Ethelbert'). Aethelbert was King of Kent only. There followed, famously, Edwin as King of Northumbria and Offa of Mercia (he of the dyke, c.783), not long before the start of the Danish invasions.

The first Danish raids are recorded in AD 787. The Danes destroyed the abbey at Lindisfarne in 793 and sacked Iona in 795. Invasions confused the picture we may have of monarchy. The king was not always 'home-grown', and could easily be found as the son of a marriage between a Briton and a Scandinavian—and, later, in the seventeenth century for example, imported from continental Europe. But it is at this point, with the invasion of the Danes, that we see one of the characteristics of monarchy: the emergence of a form of kingship in eighth-century England.

In its very simplest form, kingship is a promise by a monarch to protect the people from military intruders both from other parts of the islands as well as abroad and, importantly, from the excess of what we would come to call government. The concept of kingship existed in mythical and spiritual as well as tribal societies many centuries earlier, and in more complex form in other societies, especially in Asia and the Middle East, than the example given for our purposes.[7] Here was arguably a transition from pagan worship to Christianity endorsed by the minor monarchies.

With the emergence of kingship and a new threat whose ferocity had barely been before witnessed—if we date the start of the Danish raids from the late 780s AD—it is not unreasonable that the scattered and

---

[7] For the complexities in this subject, see Porteous, Norman Walker, *The Kingship of God in Pre-Exilic Hebrew Religion* (*Lectiones in Vetere Testamento et rebus judaicis*), no.3, 1939 and Cheney, William, *The Cult of Kingship in Anglo-Saxon England: The Transition from Paganism to Christianity*, Manchester University Press, 1970.

independently minded Britons from disparate origins began to come together under a single leader. So it was in 829. Other kings recognised Egbert, for more than a quarter of a century the increasingly powerful King of Wessex, as overlord of England. But he was still not King of England. Most certainly he did not govern England. In fact, so powerful were the Danes that they overran almost the whole of East Anglia, which had a good coastline for them, with its shallow, sloping shore that beached their vessels with fewer risks than the cliff shores elsewhere on the eastern seaboard, especially those further north. So sure were the Danes that in 876 they were able to establish their own kingdom, York, portion Mercia and take London. It was Alfred, who had become King of Wessex in 871, who led the army that got back what was to be England's capital. Kings last for just brief moments in history. By 899, Alfred was gone and the now much underrated Edward the Elder, Alfred's son, became King of Wessex in Alfred's stead.

Edward the Elder reigned twenty-five years and set the terms of territorial mastery that would later in the century make possible a king of England and not just an overlord. This was another example of the distinction of being monarch of the people or monarch of the land, in which not only the English lived but others too, for many raiders came and stayed. This was an England with Britons of far Wessex and Cornwall; the English of Wessex, Essex, Sussex, Middlesex, Anglia, Mercia and Northumberland; and the issue of one-time invaders who had remained as an émigré part of the land. The land was a country that became a state with an identity, with a monarch who reflected the identity of his people. Edward the Elder, although never to be King of Britain or even England, manoeuvred his armies and coffers, and successfully brought all the Danish lands beneath a line roughly from the Wash to the Severn within his realm. That was all he could manage. Though he had authority in Wales, he had no resources to be confident of control and most certainly he could never expect to control Mercia. Vast tracks of land had to be marched through, with uncertain supply lines, quickly changing loyalties among those to be faced and, too often, among those who marched behind.

Even when territory was taken, the hardest task of a campaign could easily be maintaining the logistical supply, loyalties, the need and desire of even loyal foot soldiers to return home, and the uncertainties of leaving a rearguard and holding army to maintain that which had been secured at an often high cost. This was not a time when reinforcements, relief supplies and soldiers could be drafted in at a few days' notice. Taking and holding territory within a king's own island was never to be a guarantee of peace to come for very long. We might remember that in the tenth century, without the majority of the lords' and magnates' commitment to the throne, no monarch had the money, military or patronage to rule beyond his regional and tribal homeland. The recognition that at least most of the resources were in place, and the gathering of regional and outside support, did not gather in place in England until the tenth century, and the reigns of Athelstan and Edgar.

Athelstan's reign reminds us how 'international' the dealings and therefore the pressures confronting leaders and monarchs of the period were. Even the *Anglo-Saxon Chronicle*—not a fan of Athelstan—shows how the need to conquer the islands also meant the need to subdue the ambitions of those outside Britain, as well as those within.[8] Athelstan came to the English throne in AD 925, although there are references to his father, Edward the Elder, dying the previous year, in 924. The blood succession is important. Athelstan was the grandson of Alfred the Great. He was no ordinary prince. Imagine what that lineage would have meant in tenth-century England. Alfred the Great, so supreme a king, that the very name and image inspired loyalty, and fear in others.[9] After all, he remains the only English monarch to be given the title 'Great'.

Alfred was far more than a warrior. His burnt-cakes and sword-swinging image suggest that Alfred is not always remembered as the

[8] The *Anglo-Saxon Chronicle* is the single most important source of Britain's history and language during the period that carries its name. There are nine chronicles, collectively known as the 'Anglo-Saxon Chronicle' and individually called after their monastic identification: Winchester, Abingdon, Worcester and Canterbury; the earliest date is 60 BC and the last AD 1154. The first chronicle was authored in Wessex during the reign of Alfred the Great and in some senses it is the beginning of the notion that the origins of the work reflect eulogistic nature towards that king. There are surviving fragments in the British Library in London, in the Parker Library at Corpus Christi, Cambridge, and two in the Bodleian at Oxford.

[9] Alfred the Great lived from AD 849–99 and was King of Wessex from 871–99.

important British lawmaker that he was. Yet his Book of Dooms (dooms are judgements) is the basis for what became English Common Law. We might note that the first church in England was built in AD 166, at Glastonbury—very much a Wessex community. Alfred became King of Wessex in 871. Given the influence of Christian thought and principle for some seven hundred years by the time Alfred succeeded Aethelred, it was not surprising that jurisprudence might reflect a biblical code. Alfred's Book of Dooms acknowledged the Ten Commandments as a source of Anglo-Saxon law and the administration of the people. A constant theme in the Book of Dooms is part-biblical credo: do unto others as you would have them do unto you. This leads to a very recognisable Alfredian notion that there should not be one law for friends and another for enemies, and, therefore, to the principle of the spirit of mercy that allows a pragmatic interval (but not a conclusion) in Anglo-Danish warfare.[10] Giving to his people laws and judgements meant Alfred was governing how they and visitors (welcome or otherwise) to the population would be controlled within the law.

Alfred's laws set moral, civil and judicial boundaries on society so that national, regional and local authority might be safeguarded. Moreover, once clearly established, these identified those whom it judged to be outside the law. Alfred's tenth-century judgements were thus models for twenty-first-century jurisprudence. From this we see that the pedigree from Alfred, although brutally soiled with the times, illustrated the developing needs, promises and ambitions of kingship, and, therefore, of monarchy over vaster territory than just regional domains by the tenth century. Into this important, constitutionally sensitive era in England's monarchy strode Alfred the Great's grandson, Athelstan. For the first time England would be ruled as one state; until this point the king ruled either a region or, at most, the English people, but not the lands in which they lived and in which others, particularly the Danes, also lived.

In AD 899, Athelstan's father, Edward the Elder (Alfred's son),

---

[10] The Book of Dooms, probably compiled c.890, came from a collection of three similar books of judgement, dating first from Aethelberht of Kent three hundred years earlier, then from Ine of Wessex two hundred years earlier, and finally from the work of the more famous Offa of Mercia c.786.

became King of Wessex. He defeated the Danes at York, but it was not until 918 that he managed to overrun Mercia and join it with Wessex. Given his strengths and the geography of his titles, Edward the Elder almost immediately convinced the warring princes in Wales that he was their overlord—not king, but a lord over them. Quickly, the kings of York, Strathclyde and Scotia paid similar allegiance. But allegiance is fickle at any moment in history. In tenth-century England, where neighbours exercised jealousies as well as promises, allegiances could easily fade and did so; and in 924, when Edward the Elder died and Athelstan came to his throne, his inheritance, while strongly defined and administered, was vulnerable to those jealousies that would unseat his authority.

In spite of all this and partly because the heritage of his grandfather and father, Athelstan established the first monarchy of all England. He was not a man who would rule with barely sheathed sword and cleverly deployed armies, even though it is the success of his armour by which he is mostly remembered. Two years into his reign, Athelstan swept the Danes from their northern stronghold, York, then threatened and subdued the other northern kings and, importantly, Constantine, King of the Scots ('of the Scots', not 'of Scotland', is correct appellation for that country's ruler). This was by some reasoning simply recapturing territory and allegiances, as Edward the Elder had also forced the Scots and the northern princes and kings to recognise his overlordship. We must not think of Athelstan as a lone figure waiting for his time to come. He fought alongside his father, then as prince and leader. Within months of his coronation, Athelstan's sword was drawn and remained rarely hidden for the rest of his reign.

The *Anglo-Saxon Chronicle* tells us that soon after Athelstan became King of Mercia he gave his sister to Otho, son of the King of the Old Saxons, thus, he hoped, securing a peace between the two men. This was in AD 925, the year that Dunstan (later Saint Dunstan) was born. The following year, Athelstan took Northumbria and established the greatest possible authority available to him. He 'governed all the kings that were in this island: Howel, King of West Wales; and Constantine, King of the Scots; and Owen, King of Monmouth; and Aldred, the son of Eadulf, of Bamburgh. And with covenants and oaths they ratified their agreement in the place called Emmet, on the fourth day before the ides of July; and renounced all idolatry, and afterwards returned in peace.'

The great battle of Athelstan's time was yet to come. It was AD 937, and we would do well to ponder the unrelenting brutality and the manner in which he and his brother, Edmund, defeated the Picts and Scots of Constantine II and Owen I of Strathclyde, the Danes, the ferocious Irish Norsemen led by Olaf III Guthfrithson, and the northern princes at the Battle of Brunanburh. We really do not know the exact location of Brunanburh, but we do have in the *Anglo-Saxon Chronicle* the text of this dreadful meeting of swords and revenge in what surely is the first epic poem in English literature:

In this year King Aethelstan, Lord of Earls, ring-giver to men, and his brother also, Prince Eadmund, won eternal glory in battle with sword edges around Brunanburh. They split the shield-wall, they hewed battle shields with the remnants of hammers. The sons of Eadweard, it was only befitting their noble descent from their ancestors that they should often defend their land in battle against each hostile people, horde and home. The enemy perished, Scots men and seamen, fated they fell. The field flowed with blood of warriors, from sun up in the morning, when the glorious star glided over the earth, God's bright candle, eternal lord, till that noble creation sank to its seat. There lay many a warrior by spears destroyed; Northern men shot over shield, likewise Scottish as well, weary, war sated.

The West-Saxons pushed onward all day; in troops they pursued the hostile people. They hewed the fugitive grievously from behind with swords sharp from the grinding. The Mercians did not refuse hard hand-play to any warrior who came with Anlaf over the sea-surge in the bosom of a ship, those who sought land, fated to fight. Five lay dead on the battle-field, young kings, put to sleep by swords, likewise also seven of Anlaf's earls, countless of the army, sailors and Scots. There the Northmen's chief was put to flight, by need constrained to the prow of a ship with little company: he pressed the ship afloat, the king went out on the dusky flood-tide, he saved his life. Likewise, there also the old campaigner—Constantine, hoary warrior—through flight came to his own region in the north. He had no reason to exult the great meeting; he was of his kinsmen bereft, friends fell on the battle-field, killed at strife: even his son, young in battle, he left in the place of slaughter, ground to pieces with wounds. That grizzle-haired warrior had no reason to boast of sword-slaughter, old deceitful one, no more did Anlaf; with their remnant of an army they had no reason to laugh that they were better in deed of war in battle-field—collision of banners, encounter of spears, encounter of men, trading of blows—when they played against the sons of Eadweard on the battle-field.

Departed then the Northmen in nailed ships. The dejected survivors of the battle, sought Dublin over the deep water, to return to Ireland, ashamed in spirit. Likewise the brothers, both together, King and Prince, sought their home, West-Saxon land, exultant from battle. They left behind them, to enjoy the corpses, the dark-coated one, the dark horny-beaked raven and the dusky-coated one, the eagle white from behind, to partake of carrion, greedy war-hawk, and that grey animal the wolf in the forest.

Never was there more slaughter on this island, never yet as many people killed before this with sword's edge: never according to those who tell us from books, old wisemen, since from the east Angles and Saxons came up over the broad sea. Britain they sought, proud war-smiths who overcame the Welsh, glorious warriors they took hold of the land.

There was never more 'slaughter on this island, never yet as many killed with sword's edge'. Those left on the field of Brunanburh were pecked and shredded by raven and wolf. Thus Athelstan conquered the land of the English. The killing done but the swords unsheathed, Athelstan scrutinised the laws, codes and judgements of his grandfather and father, and revised them to cope with his increased authority. His means encouraged the scattered to come to the villages until they became towns, so business could only be conducted in those small towns, encouraging them to grow and form the basis of urban living that would see the beginnings of places and names that would be strengthened by the thirteenth and fourteenth centuries, until the island urban identity was strong enough to survive in the twenty-first century. We may assume urban and city communities and conurbations to be products of Victorian industrial revolution,

Athelstan, the first king of the *state* of England,
ruled 924–39.

but in truth the majority of rural and even urban townships were
identifiable in the Middle Ages, and in turn many of those had their
origins in the Saxon societies created before the coming of William
of Normandy.

> AD 941. This year King Athelstan died in Glocester, on the sixth
> day before the calends of November, about forty-one winters,
> bating one night, from the time when King Alfred died. And
> Edmund Atheling took to the kingdom. He was then eighteen
> years old. King Athelstan reigned fourteen years and ten weeks.
> This year the Northumbrians abandoned their allegiance, and
> chose Anlaf of Ireland for their king.[11]

---

[11] From the Reverend James Ingram's translation of the *Anglo-Saxon Chronicle*, to be
seen in the Lillian Goldman Law Library at the Yale Law School.

These were the times and here is a simple example in British history where even a major event cannot be seen as set in stone. This was Saxon England. It was a land still learning the uncompromising ways of government. Government was an extension of kingship. Kingship had its origins in religious authority. It offered to protect the people in return for their allegiance. It all sounded, or sounds now, perfectly reasonable. In uncertain times, when boundaries were protected only by the power of the leaders within those boundaries ruthlessly to deal with trespassers, the balance between allegiance and protection was difficult to maintain—for either party. As the Anglo-Saxon chronicler tells us above, when Athelstan, who had conquered the whole of England and had the allegiance of all its leaders and those in Scotland and Wales, died, his half-brother Edmund Atheling, just eighteen, was unable to command immediate respect and so 'the Northumbrians abandoned their allegiance, and chose Anlaf of Ireland for their king'. Effectively, Edmund had lost the north. England, the state, no longer had a king. Edmund spent most of his short reign (AD 939–46) recovering his lands. In 944 he regained Mercia, held by the Danes, and then savagely slashed his way to Strathclyde. Battleaxing monarchs might often be remembered for far more contemplative achievements. So it is with Edmund I, because he was the first English king to promote the idea of tenth-century monastic reform.

Monasticism, the giving up of everyday and not necessarily religious life—secularism—by both men and women who entered monastic and conventual life, had existed in the British islands since the sixth century. The Iona community, founded by Columba in AD 563, became the Celtic missionary society to convert much of the north, which is the origin of Lindisfarne. The Viking-Danish invaders sacked the monasteries, although not for any unforgiving religious motive. The monasteries were simply there, with possible booty, as well as a refuge for defenders. Not unnaturally the monastic life lay low. When we get to the tenth-century times of Edmund and soon the remarkable Edgar, the revival and renewal of the monasteries began. It was monarchy that allowed and encouraged this renewal, and it was therefore an important reminder that the power of the monarch was then (and in some respects remains today) a reflection of persuasion and instinct. If Edmund or Edgar had been indifferent or certainly against the revival, it would not have taken place. Monasticism was a powerful element in the construction of a full state monarchy, particularly as the kings understood themselves to have a manageable relationship with the concept of right and wrong as suggested in Christian teaching. The biblical influence on the judgements and laws of England would hence be a long-standing reference for British rulers long after the Saxon kings had gone. Ironically, perhaps, when the monasteries had grown rich and powerful, it was a theologically inquisitive monarch, Henry VIII, who divested them of their powers and considerable treasures.[12]

If Edgar (c.AD 942–75) is to have a significant place in any history of British monarchy, it is by the considerable act of becoming monarch of the state rather than just the people. A fanciful illustration of his power is the surely apocryphal story that after his coronation at Bath, Edgar travelled north to the monastery of Saint John the Baptist on the River Dee, and was borne there by a barge rowed by eight Scottish and Welsh minor kings. Edgar, hardly the image of the Saxon battle giant— according to William of Malmesbury, he appears to have been a 'sorry little fellow' probably less than five feet tall—became king at the age of sixteen on the death of his elder brother, Edwy (sometimes known as Eadwig). Edwy had opposed and exiled Dunstan (c.925–88), the some-time abbot of Glastonbury, in c.956.

Edwy was ignored by the greater lords and regional princes, and never ruled much of England other than the easily defended region south of the River Thames. Edgar, even in his teens, had the task of re-establishing the throne's authority. He brought back Dunstan and created him Archbishop of Canterbury, and made Oswald Archbishop

---

[12] The nursery rhyme, 'Little Jack Horner', is a reference to the Dissolution of the Monasteries. 'Little Jack Horner sat in the corner eating a Christmas pie; he put in his thumb and took out a plum and said, "What a good boy am I".' At the Dissolution, the then Abbot of Glastonbury, Richard Whiting, sent his steward, Horner, to London with a pie. Inside were the deeds and titles to a number of Somerset manors. Horner is said to have opened the Christmas pie and taken the deeds to Mells manor, including the prosperous lead mines. The manor was a plum indeed, but so is the reference to the lead mines (plumbum). The Horners and their descendants, including a line to the Bonham-Carters, have lived at Mells ever since.

of Winchester, then of York. Under Edgar, the rule of the monarch increased and the land was easier.

Edgar became known as Edgar the Peaceful. His private life was anything but content. He divorced his wife to marry his mistress and took another mistress, Wulfrida, who at the very least was a novice in the convent at Wilton. The abbot insisted that he do seven years' penance, which he minded very little. He served his nation and its state for little time, and died at the age of thirty-three, to be buried at Glastonbury Abbey. Edgar's legacy for our purpose is that it was he who, after the uncertainties of the followers of Athelstan, established in England the monarchy over the whole state, which it remained apart from an interruption during the Commonwealth in the mid-seventeenth century. In the twenty-first, Edgar should still be honoured, for it was he who understood better than any monarch that to rule the whole land it was necessary to institute safe and loyal regional government. To make that work, it was Edgar who created the system of shires and thus the county system.

CHAPTER TWO

The Road to Hastings

I n Saxon England, it would seem obvious that only a monarch could
   make radical changes; but we should not dismiss past kings and
queens as simple historical, however relevant, milestones. The British
monarchy created what the United Kingdom might be today. Edgar
was as relevant as Victoria, Edward, the two Georges and Elizabeth II,
perhaps more so. That has to be understood to sense that the deeper
importance of monarchy goes far beyond the twenty-first-century
mantra, 'Is the monarchy worth it?' It is self-evident that monarchs
believe they are 'worth it'. In times past and times present, the power of
absolute patronage of the great institutions makes each one reliant on
the other, and so the whole became and becomes totally self-fulfilling.

The patronage that appoints, say, a judge who in turn appoints a silk
who in turns appoints a clerk who in turn appoints a junior counsel to
a brief is no more powerful patronage than the estate manager who
employs the lawnsman who employs the molecatcher who employs
the gunny-sack boy. Imagine what would be at stake in the gift of the
monarch and, therefore, the determination of those with an unquestionable interest in maintaining that monarch as the authority for
the distribution of layered patronage—the most convertible form of
currency. In the final years of Saxon monarchy, when the expression of
kingship took precedence over every form of patronage, the right king

at the right moment was in so many interests (and would be until the end of the coming of the first Stuart monarch of both Scotland and England in 1603) that a real or wondered-at constitutional ruthlessness was of little surprise. So it was with the last of the Danish and Saxon kings of England in the first six decades of the eleventh century that led to the last successful invasion of the British Isles.

At the centre of the change in monarchy and rebellion were the Godwines, a ruthless family with no royal lineage; yet they virtually ruled the kingdom of Edward the Confessor, who, in spite of his lapses of authority that allowed the Godwines such power, was to be one of the most famous ever rulers of the British Isles. Not surprisingly, the Godwines were the most powerful family in England in the mid-eleventh century. They were even more powerful than the kings themselves—even, at times, Cnut—because the Godwines held together the political factions that in spite of patronage the monarchs could never surely guarantee. The most powerful of the Godwines was not, in retrospect, Harold II, who would die at the Battle of Hastings, but his father, Godwine, Earl of Wessex (died 1053). Godwine was created Earl of Wessex by King Cnut (994–1035). He had two ambitions: to marry his daughter to the future king, Edward (c.1003–1066), and eventually to have a Godwine on the throne of England. He succeeded in both. In 1042, with much connivance by the Earl of Wessex and Edward's mother, the widow of Aethelred the Unready, Emma of Normandy, Edward, having lived in exile, became King of England. Two years later, he married Godwine's daughter, Edith. From that point, the Godwine family virtually ruled the kingdom.

Edward and his closest Court, understanding how much power was being stripped from the throne, began loading the highest positions with Normans; this was the origin of Duke William's claim that it was Edward who had promised him the English crown.

There was a brief confrontation that may have changed the power lines in favour of Edward when he was persuaded in 1051 to send the Godwines into exile. It was an unworkable decision and within months the Godwines, who had not lost their influences while away, were back in England. Edward spent more and more time at his devotions, not of earthly, but of heavenly reconciliation and confession, and thus increasingly allowed England to be run by the earls, including of course Wessex, who, by 1053, after the death of his father and disgrace of his elder brother, was Harold Godwineson—the future but short-lived king.

Harold, having been forcibly detained in Normandy by its duke, William, is said to have promised to help the Normans gain the English throne. There has never been proof of this story, although its importance to the tale of monarchy is that the throne could be bargained for, promised and of course fought over. There was no formal and constitutional right of succession. Whatever the basis of William of Normandy's ambition, it was immediately exercised in 1066 upon the death of the supposedly pious Edward, later known as Edward the Confessor.

Edward's image as a holy prince and monarch may have been drawn by those who, a hundred years after his death, would have had Pope Alexander III create him a saint at a time when the English throne wished to be restored in favour of the popes, after Henry II's schism with the Church following the murder of Thomas à Becket in his own cathedral at Canterbury. Nevertheless, Edward was the founder of Westminster Abbey and was even patron saint of England until 1350, when the then monarch, Edward III, wanted a more robust image than an albino of great piety for his standard bearers of war, and proclaimed the mythical Turk, George, as inspiration for English soldiers in pursuit of their own dragons. Curiously, the image of the very real Edward has survived with more credibility. Perhaps one reason that the English rarely celebrate their saint's day is that unlike the Welsh, Irish and Scots patrons—holy men and blessed therefore by the Churches of the British islanders—George has never been believable and thus matters little, especially among people of increasingly mixed beliefs or of none whatsoever.

Edward died in January 1066. He was sixty-three and had been crowned King of England in 1043 after the death of Cnut's son, King Harthacnut, and so restored the Wessex throne over England, after Danish reign (1016–42). Harold Godwineson was crowned on 6 January at Westminster and the Treasury was seized. It was never likely to have been a gentle reign and so not a long one. This was Harold II. The first Harold was Harold Harefoot (c.1015–40), who came to the throne by chance. He was Cnut's son, although Court politicians said, without any historically sound proof, that he was a bastard, and when his father died and the legitimate heir, Harthacnut, King of Denmark, was away defending that place from the Norwegians and Swedes, Harold became regent. There was another claimant, Alfred the Atheling, who at the instigation of his mother, the quite extraordinary Emma of Normandy, arrived from Normandy to usurp Harold Harefoot's claim to the throne. He did not travel well. He was murdered under the likely direction of the Godwines: captured, then blinded through to his brains. His mother, Emma, daughter of Duke Richard I of Normandy (933–96),[1] was a remarkable powerbroker. She was the wife of two kings: the first was Aethelred the Unready (1002–16); immediately on Aethelred's death, she married Cnut (1017–35). She was also the mother of two kings, Edward the Confessor (Aethelred the Unready's son), and Harthacnut (Cnut's son).

However, at this stage, even Emma could not dislodge Harold Harefoot and, in 1037, after two years as standing in as monarch, Harold was recognised as king, although his mother, Aelgifu of Northampton, may have exercised the real power. Harthacnut (and his mother Emma) were not much pleased. Harthacnut began to mass his Danes to claim his English throne. There was no battle. Harold Harefoot, Harold I of England, died on 17 March 1040. His body was taken to Westminster Abbey and interred, but hardly laid to rest. That summer, Harthacnut claimed the throne of England, and had Harold I's body dug up, beheaded and thrown into a bog. The remains were rescued from ignominy by the late king's followers and reburied at Saint Clement Danes, near the Thames in London. In the twentieth century, it became the church of the Royal Air Force—an irony given that Pope Clement was a patron saint of seafarers. (Clement was the fourth pope and his martyrdom followed after he was bound to an anchor and cast into the sea.) Why Danes? The Thames's north shore was home to a colony of Danish mariners.

Harold Godwineson, Harold II, was the first king of England to be killed in battle. Richard I, from gangrene after being shot by a cross-bowman during the siege of Châlus (1199), and Richard III at Bosworth Field (1485) were the only others. Harold II died on 14 October 1066 defending his throne and thus the kingdom against the last successful

---

[1] a.k.a. 'sans peur', the Fearless.

invader. Three weeks earlier, at the Battle of Stamford Bridge,[2] seven miles to the east of York on the Derwent River, he fought his exiled half-brother, Tostig, and Harold Hadraada, King of Norway, whose invading army of as many as fifteen thousand men had sailed from Norway in a fleet of three hundred ships to seize England. On that day, 25 September 1066, Harold II killed both his brother and Hadraada.

The slaughter of the unsuspecting Norse army was horrific. The survivors needed but twenty-four of their three hundred ships to carry them north to the Orkney Islands and then to Norway. Harold II's triumph had little moment for celebration. On 28 September, with his largely exhausted army still camped in the East Riding, news came that William of Normandy had landed on the shallow, sloping beaches at Pevensey on the English Channel coast. Harold buried his dead and began his forced march along the 185 miles to London and then sixty miles more south from his capital to face the Normans at Senlac Hill, six or so miles inland from the fishing village of Hastings.

The Norman host won the day and Saxon England died. Its kings achieved much and were the guardians of kingship. Its peoples spoke a similar language and were ruled in that tongue. Codes and human protocols were understood. But Saxon rule was no more. Now came the Normans, ruling by the conjugations of their own ways of government, written and construed in what would come to be understood as French and Latin scripts. A nation knows itself by its tongue. It is the only sure identity. It would take time, more than decades, even centuries, but with the death of Harold Godwineson, the British and their way of monarchy took on a new personality. Saxon England had been only a bit of timeline.

Duke William was King of England and in theory Britain was now Norman; but Saxons did not simply disappear on 15 October 1066. In England, William never truly ruled. He had the south, but there were parts of the rest of the kingdom—especially the further north his soldiers travelled—that he would never expect to hold. This was just the second half of the eleventh century. There were the logistical

---

[2] In 1066, this was stone, ford and bridge across the Derwent. There was no hamlet or village of that name.

difficulties: the lack of communications and of a municipal and constitutional wiring diagram that would hopefully have allowed Saxons to
be removed and Normans to take over; there was not least the ability
to take an area, but the uncertainty of holding it once your main army
moved on. William never entirely trusted his own factions.[3] To take a
kingdom did not mean it could be held. For some time after the invasion
and the way to conquest, Britain could be seen as a miniature version
of twenty-first-century Afghanistan. The nominal leader of the disparate opposition to William was commanded by Edgar the Aetheling,
the surviving son of the Confessor and supported by Ealdred, the
powerful Archbishop of York. It was not much of a protest. It never
could be. Moreover, it fulfilled the notion of the authors of The Anglo-
Saxon Chronicle that the invasion had succeeded as God's punishment
for Saxon ways. Everything very neatly tied up, but that did not mean
the Saxon fidelity to times and instincts by would disappear.

During the autumn of 1066 the last of the Saxon kings perished, but
Anglo-Saxons did not. The character and image of the Saxons would to
a degree exist in the British people and their notion of monarchy for a
thousand years to come. Even in the twentieth and twenty-first centuries, the United Kingdom's continental European political and economic
critics (including General Charles de Gaulle) still referred to 'Anglo-
Saxon' attitudes in British corridors of assumed power. Moreover,
American governing and influential élites are still referred to as WASPS:
White Anglo-Saxon Protestants.

---

[3] For example, the Norman knights who would eventually rule Pembrokeshire were
ever feared as having too much power. In the twelfth century, it was these knights who
were sent to 'rescue' the monarchy of Ireland and had Henry II concerned that they
were setting up their own kingdom.

CHAPTER THREE

Norman Rule and Beyond

T he steadfastness of monarchy is much tested during its opening
moments; at this time the monarch must sense the hope of his
or her people that they will be quietly governed; that is, without fuss
and alarm.[1] There was no orderly transition from Saxon to Norman
monarch. The fact that William quickly needed to build castles
(Hastings, Dover, London, Lincoln, York, Nottingham, Durham) to
defend his positions demonstrated his insecurities and hold witness
to the seven often numbingly cruel years that it took to subjugate
Britain.[2] At first, William had thought he had much of the country more
or less in his control. He did not, because his resources were too scattered and many of the powerful magnates had not retreated before his

[1] *The Book of Common Prayer*: 'The prayer for the Whole State of Christ's Church
Militant Here on Earth... save and defend all Christian Kings, Princes, and Governors;
and specially thy servant *ELIZABETH* our Queen; that under her we may be godly and
quietly governed.'
[2] These were not huge stone affairs, but wooden buildings built atop large mounds
(*mottes*) with a stock (bailey—hence Old Bailey) at the mound's base. The structure
was called a motte and bailey castle, and was the makeshift structure until a perma-
nent castle could be started, as at Hastings, Dover and Durham, and, most famously,
in the form of the Tower of London.

Hastings Castle a few miles from the inland battleground built
by William the Conqueror, part destroyed by King John and rebuilt by
Henry III in 1220.

Norman advance. Many of them, especially the old established Danes
were convinced that William could be sent in retreat to Normandy.
Therefore, it was not possible to declare that, with William's successful
invasion, the death of Harold II and his own coronation, all was immediately settled.

At his coronation on Christmas Day 1066, William, under the guidance of his archbishop, Ealdred, promised that he would properly and
quietly govern the people as long as they would promise their allegiance—the Saxon concept of kingship and the promise of the great
King Cnut. However, with the judgement of an invading prince and
once again foreign rule, here in the eleventh century there would
appear to be some obligation of a monarch to recognise and protect
fundamental freedoms of the people. In very broad terms, the upholder
of kingship was, even in Saxon-Norman times, the guardian of human
rights, however loosely and precariously defined. William returned
to Normandy three months after his coronation, taking with him the

most important Saxon magnates who otherwise might have fostered an uprising.

The *Anglo-Saxon Chronicle* noted that William's half-brother, Bishop Odo of Bayeux (who ordered the stitching and sewing of the famous tapestry), set out with his lieutenants, including the cruel William FitzOsbern, to harass 'the miserable people'. The eleventh-century monk, Oderic Vitalis, wrote in *Historia ecclesiastica* that William yielded to his worst impulse and set no bounds to his fury, condemning the innocent and the guilty to a common fate.[3] Talk of human rights and kingship may be far-fetched. Yet given the times, and the terrible and bloody way of rule and its enforcement, there remained an obligation of sorts that would recognise kingship. Certainly, when that obligation lapsed at times throughout the Middle Ages, it was because the monarch was weak and the people were no longer quietly governed; it was often a moment for the king's enemies (including his family, as in William of Normandy's case) to pounce.

There was one faction, in truth an institution, that monarchs needed to keep on side—even more so than warring families. This was the Church. When the Christian Church arrived in Britain, its first purpose was conversion and the first convert was always the monarch. Without the monarch's blessing, Church missionaries—including he who would be remembered as Saint Augustine—would be declared enemies of the state. They would be seen and heard as terrorists spreading an alternative authority to the monarch. As the Church became powerful, especially in continental Europe, the monarch needed the Church. When William of Normandy planned his invasion he managed to persuade his supporters to convince the pope, Alexander II, to give his blessing to the campaign; when William's men scaled Senlac Hill to destroy the Saxons, they were led by the banners of Normandy and Rome. Victory seized, two of Alexander's cardinals were in England to give William a second coronation, and make sure that William and Church stood shoulder to shoulder in the decimation of the English

---

[3] For a comprehensive history of sixty years of the post-invasion history of Saxon-Norman England, see Dr Marjorie Chibnall's six-volume translation of *Historia ecclesiastica*, which first appeared in 1969.

Church. Unsurprisingly, it was seen as an institution of dissenters and packed with Saxons; William and the Holy Father's emissaries rid it of both. In doing so, they perhaps did good service to the Church that was in England. Importantly for our modern story, here were the practical beginnings of the unbreakable authority of the British monarch over the Church. The king would of course recognise the ultimate authority of God and his Vicar on Earth. Equally importantly, the king would rule the Church in these islands. Henry VIII was not the first to fashion it to his own ways.

The tenth and eleventh centuries see the establishment of the unrelenting authority of British monarchy, based on three elements: kingship, Christianity and the constitutional peculiarity of being an island race. This last point is obviously too easily forgotten. The three oldest surviving monarchies are Japan's, Denmark's and what is now the United Kingdom's. Each is small enough for a monarchy and, in modern times, its democratic administrators to govern. The two island peoples have even simpler credentials for monarchy. Unlike continental states, island nations do not have histories of alien armies crisscrossing them, easily pillaging almost everything but identity along the way. Again, therefore, monarchy reflects a nation's identity more than a governing republican. Does this mean that, say, the British identity was laid down by Athelstan and Edgar's Saxons, and confirmed by William's Normans? Probably so. Everything that followed built on that period, right up to the twenty-first century, even though the monarch has only imagined political power.

The Normans created feudal England and knighthoods. Before William of Normandy arrived at Pevensey, feudalism existed only in continental Europe and there was no title of 'knight' in Saxon Britain, although a mercenary young servant was known in Saxon English as a *cniht*, but no order of chivalry existed. The Germans had a knight figure called a *kneht* and in Dutch it would have been *knecht*. The Iranian Sarmatians had mounted horsemen of special breeding and deed, and this was a general acceptance of a knight's status; this was certainly true by the time of the ninth-century Frankish figure and *pater Europae*, Emperor Charlemagne (AD 742–842). But most of this passed the British island people by— then, as now, they had no deep interest in a united Europe.

It was from this same period, about the eighth century, that the bond of feudalism grew in continental Europe. Today, 'feudalism' is used as a pejorative term, yet its origins in Frankish Europe were an inevitable and often progressive social system where none other was offered. In its crudest form, feudalism was a way in which those who had land had on it tenants, who, by promises of military as well as agricultural servitude, paid more than dues and duties. The tenancy could sometimes be inherited. It was also the case that the tenancies were linked to the legality of holding for no more than the lifetime of the worker. It was, in effect, a benefice. It was the basis of this system that became British feudalism and it was introduced from continental Europe by the Normans.

> It is the custom in England, as in other countries, for the nobility to have great power over the common people, who are their serfs. This means that they are bound by law and custom to plough the fields of their masters, harvest the corn, gather it into barns, and thresh and winnow the grain; they must also mow and carry home the hay, cut and collect wood, and perform all manner of tasks of this kind.[4]

Once in the British Isles, the system developed in a different direction, and became a formal system under royal and manorial patronage that would survive well into the fourteenth century. Yet elements of feudalism continued by custom and convenience, even if they held little sympathy in law. Given that all that passes does not pass away, in the twenty-first century there is to be found a sense of feudalism in some tenancies beneficial in those agreements, just as they were (and were not in other instances) in the developing Middle Ages. It took four years to get some sense that the Normans controlled much of England.

To protect his 'internal' borders, William created the Marcher Lords. The term comes from the Anglo-Saxon *mearc* and the Norman French *marche*, both meaning the border area between two territories. The first of the Marcher Lordships, with castle, was Hereford, and the later fourteenth-century title included that of marquess or marquis, and from that came the female title, marchioness. Thus the Norman monarchy introduced to the British Isles a new and lasting list of heraldry, if

---

[4] Froissart, Jean, *Chronicles*, c.1395.

not chivalry. These titles had practical value. Their holders had to be powerful enough to defend the monarch's interests and, at the same time, not so powerful that their loyalty to the monarchy would be tested either directly or as a co-conspiracy. Reasonably, then, no monarch was safe from the feckless ambition of something quite new in British society, aristocracy in the form of knighted warriors.

A duty of monarchy is to be aware of the way and mood of his or her people; only then may the contract of kingship be honoured, and the stability of the monarch and to some extent the monarchy itself be as assured as it might ever be. When the country's mood runs ahead of the monarch's expectation, as it did against Victoria when she retreated from London in the years after Albert's death, and as it did again when Elizabeth II failed to sense the public mood in the days immediately following the death of Diana, Princess of Wales, the monarchy is at the very least vulnerable to the charge that it has lost its way.

Part of the awareness of discipline that has been one of the stones upon which the British monarchy has rested has been to know exactly what it is that the king or queen rules; the first national record of the level of awareness is perhaps the single most important ledger in the legacy of William of Normandy as King of England: the Domesday Book. After the Conquest, William proclaimed all the land in England as his own. He kept some twenty per cent of it as king's land and for his use only. Part of the way in which he could (and had to) repay the magnates—some 170— who had travelled with him from Normandy with their own armies was to give them the tenancy of great swathes of land. It was the finest booty of war on which they could establish their own baronies and it was, they believed, only right, as Earl Warrenne declaimed when he produced his sword, to show by what right he settled his manor:

> Look at this, my lords, this is my warrant! For my ancestors came with William and conquered their lands with the sword, and by the sword I will defend them from anyone intending to seize them. The king did not conquer and subject the land by himself, but our forebears were sharers and partners with him.[5]

---

[5] Walter of Guisborough, *Chronicle of Walter of Hemingford*, c.1310.

Page from Domesday Book for Bedfordshire—part of the survey of
Britain by William of Normandy in 1086.

They built their manors and their castles, and, as they had in part
return to provide the king's army with mounted knights, soon, through
patronage of the king, then the barons, then the knights, there were
some 6,000 important and minor manors and tenancies developed in
what had once been Saxon England. These invaded and grabbed swathes
were soon administered as settlements, and the administration and
judgements (dooms) were in Norman French, as were the hearings and
commission courts sent throughout William's kingdom. Because the
commissions sat jointly with Saxons, albeit placemen in many cases, it
was soon understood that once a judgement or doom had been made,
there was no appeal. It was all in the Domesday books and there that
judgement would remain.

The Domesday books (the Little Domesday covered Essex, Norfolk
and Suffolk, and the main Domesday Book much of the rest of England)
are a list of property and holdings in the year 1086—other than the
Treasury cities of London and Winchester—south of the Ribble and
Tees rivers, the then border between Scotland and England. Each of the
regions and shires was surveyed by commissioners who set up boards in
the shire courts to produce records for 13,418 places, from settlements
to towns. The commissioners gathered the names of landholders (not
necessarily the same as landowners) and of who cultivated the land,
the acreage and what could be tilled, grown or grazed on each holding.
Here is an example in modern transliteration from the Little Domesday
that surveys Norfolk. The reference to King Edward is Edward the
Confessor—a reminder that William was not the first to produce a
record of a parish:

> Scerpham Hundred Culverstestun. Edric held it in the time of
> King Edward. Two plowlands of land. At all times there were 4
> villagers, and 1 cottager, and 4 slaves; 5 acres of meadow and
> 2 plowlands in the demesne. Then and afterwards 1 plowland,
> now one-half. At all times 1 mill and 1 fishpond. Here is located
> 1 socman of the king, of 40 acres of land; which his predeces-
> sors held only as commended and he claims his land from the
> gift of the king. Then and afterwards there was 1 plowland, now
> 2 bovates, and 2 acres of meadow. At all times 2 riding horses,
> and 4 geese; then 300 sheep, now 300 less 12; then 16 swine,

now 3. Then and afterwards it was worth 60 shillings, now 80; and there could be one plowland. Walter of Caen holds it from Robert.

Heinstede Hundred. In Sasilingaham. Edric, the predecessor of Robert Malet, held 2 jurisdictions and a half, of 66 acres of land, now Walter holds them. Then 9 cottagers, now 13. At all times 3 plowlands and a half among all, and 3 acres of meadow, and the 8th part of a mill; and under these 1 jurisdiction of 6 acres of land. At all times half a plowland. Then it was worth 30 shillings, now it returns 50 shillings.

In Scotessa Ulcetel was tenant, a free man commended to Edric, in the time of King Edward of 30 acres of land. At that time 1 cottager, afterward and now 2. Then half a plowland, none afterward nor now. It was at all times worth 5 shillings and 4 pence; the same.

The Domesday Book was the most detailed audit of the landed wealth of a nation of any European state or realm ever in the Middle Ages. Although decided by Norman masters, two pertinent points were established: first, Saxons would also sit on the commissions to help resolve disputes, but also to establish facts. Not all Saxons rebelled and went into hilltop defences. Many Saxons saw the reality of the Conquest and not unreasonably saw there was more to be gained from becoming part of the new administration of England than opposing it. The second important point is contained in the title of the survey: the doom. The doom was an instruction or an ordinance, but most of all it was a judgement and could not be appealed. In the Domesday Book lay the evidence needed to draw taxes from the people to finance the Treasury. In modern-day terms, it was the source of an unrivalled property and council tax, and thus revolutionary in the way authority could cite parish names and holdings as a bought-ledger account of where dues could be levied for the common good—that is, the good of the monarch's ambitions. For only the monarch had the authority to effect the descending order of patronage that would allow England to move into the bureaucracy (as well as the deprivations) of a European-inspired feudal system. The Norman kings strengthened the authority of the monarchy in England through the re-organised administration of the state—in Norman French and not in the still spoken Anglo-Saxon. There came, too, the reform of the Church in England (this was not the same as the Tudor creation, the Church of England), initiated as a reaction to the power amassed by the Saxon Archbishop of Canterbury, Stigand (died 1072), whom William of Normandy deposed in 1070.

The importance of Stigand at this stage of the history of the monarchy is his presence at the crossover from Saxon to Norman, and his experience as royal chaplain and confidant to Cnut, and, on his death, to that king's offspring, Harold Harefoot and Harthacnut. Thus Stigand became gatherer of enormous wealth, enough to rival the monarch's house. With it came power that was strong enough to face down the authority of the popes, who excommunicated him, which meant he had no authority to crown William, but they failed to shift his seat from Winchester and Canterbury.[6] Eventually, and because of his powerful position, Stigand was deposed by the pope's men and imprisoned. This was the signal for the Normans, whom until then Stigand had opposed, to accuse not just Stigand but the whole Church in England to be in need of complete reform. How was it that Stigand could stay in power so long after the invasion? The answer is probably in the rebellions that followed the defeat of Harold in 1066. William, to gain popular and Saxon magnate favours, had Stigand in his Court. Once the rebellions had been put down, William felt confident enough to have him sent away. Stigand understood this fall of the political dice against his further ambition. There is no outstanding ecclesiastical record in this man's favour. Stigand was an uncompromising politician dressed in cope and mitre. The importance of him in our story is to date one of the earliest examples of the leader of the English Church having a voice strong enough to be heard by the people and for the monarch, or later holder of absolute power, to listen carefully to the archbishop's tenor in his homily.

Others would soon follow Stigand and others would also perish. But from the Norman invasion onwards the Archbishop of Canterbury

---

[6] Stigand was excommunicated (or was refused permission to administer all duties and rites of a bishop) by five popes: Leo IX, Victor II, Stephen IX, Nicholas II and Alexander II. The latter's opposition to Stigand may have led to his support for William of Normandy's cause to take the English throne.

exercised more power than the size and strength of his Church appeared to justify, even in most recent years.[7] Saxon kings had to accept the need to justify their authority, and demands for allegiance and the Norman invaders had learned that the English realm was not protected by its moated distance from continental Europe. The Normans had to fight for allegiance in the revolutionary tendency of the savagely tribal provinces of England and at the same time return with haste across the English Channel to protect the dukedom in a land that was not yet France and had all the attendant disloyalties of vulnerable ambitious families. William, as an example, recognised he was more vulnerable to treachery within his own family than in the very heart of opposition in his conquered island. There was nothing but conflict in each English province; but the kingdom that was once Cnut's centre of empire was a better dukedom for the Norman.

The Normans have an important part in our story of monarchy's future. Saxon authority over the state of England has left little on the conscience of the second Elizabethan England. Yet the rapidly changing image of Norman, Angevin and Plantagenet English history is incomplete if we are to feel the indelible mark of monarchy on the character and instincts of the British Isles. What is often missing is the realisation that a form of monarchy was developing in the sometimes wild lanes abutting England, with all its domination of historical importance. The story of how and why the Welsh and Scottish princes were so very much part of the emerging story of English medieval monarchy should not be airbrushed from the bigger picture of monarchy in Britain—especially the part played by the Welsh.

[7] The Anglo-Catholic Archbishop of Canterbury Cosmo Lang (1864–1945) was one of those who brought about the abdication of King Edward VIII. In 1982 Archbishop Robert Runcie (1921–2000) refused to give a victory homily—as Prime Minister Margaret Thatcher wanted him to do—at the Saint Paul's Cathedral post-Falklands War service.

CHAPTER FOUR

The Welsh Princes and
Their Influence

W hen the too often forgotten Welsh princes established kingdoms and rule they were doing more than defending limited
tribal territory. Leadership had to take the form of kingship and therefore of authority over something that could be identified as a kingdom.
The Welsh kings—they were that rather than just princes—began to
achieve a statehood that should be remembered even in the twenty-
first century: an indelible characteristic of monarchy is for it to reflect
the identity of those who pledge allegiance. The Welsh chieftains and
greater rulers have a historical significance far bigger than what the
Welsh sometimes rightly see as crucial centuries virtually forgotten in
the record by the English, who dismiss them as interesting, but never
important. It would be good to remember that the Welsh were powerful
enough to take their place at Runnymede for the signing of Magna
Carta.[1]

The Welsh had no monarchy in the English style, although north
Wales was the kingdom of Gwynedd. They had ruling princes, all of

---

[1] 15 June 1215.

whom were natives of Wales, and who campaigned and in part ruled from the mid-eleventh century until the closing years of the thirteenth and Edward I's successful campaign against all Welsh opposition. Because of Wales's nature and its environment, the princes suffered from 'clannish' instincts and size, easily identifiable within the tapestry of the six regions of what was often forbidding military terrain in a small country.[2] Moreover, the territory had no focal point of authority. There was no central capital and even where there were strongholds of leadership many of them were impossible to get to and that made Wales even more parochial.

It may be wrong to describe medieval Wales as a country until the Edwardian conquest. Instead, it was a collection of regions and localities, of ever shifting boundaries, hegemonies and loyalties.[3] Loyalties were constantly tested and often defeated. For example, in the hundred years or so leading up to the Norman Conquest, thirty-five Welsh rulers were killed, often murdered, by their own people. From this we can perhaps see why there could have been few possibilities for establishing a national monarchy; the impression is that if they had managed to come together instead of battling their internecine wars, they might have worked an easier strategy to counter English ambitions and insecurities. Yet the Welsh leaders were by any definition powerful and often innovative people.

There were few reliable and continuous written Court records in early Wales. Much of what we read is from the eulogies of the bards and, ironically, the accounts and ledgers of their natural enemies—the English. But we can make some judgement from evidence that tribal and regional kingdom chiefs had to maintain power among their own people, many of whom spent most of their lives attempting to exist off poor land and even poorer circumstances. Like the English and Scottish leaders, the Welsh mostly faced insurrection and disloyalties from within; we know more about deeds in battle than we do about foundations of Welsh law and public administration. Until the early eighteenth

---

[2] Gwynedd Uwch Conwy, Gwynedd Is Conwy, Powys, Rhwyng Gwy a Hafren, Dyfed and Ystrad Tywi.

[3] Turvey, Roger, 'The Welsh Princes 1063–1283', in Bates, David (ed.), *The Medieval World*, Longman, Edinburgh, 2002.

century, a considerable number of rulers in the British Isles were judged by martial achievements (or otherwise).

So it was with the Welsh. Yet it was national rivalries that demonstrated these military achievements. After all, there is no evidence that the Normans or four later Plantagenet kings[4] made much effort to subdue the Welsh other than to mount twenty or so punitive expeditions between 1081 and 1267, although Henry I (1068–1135) did build a sturdy English foothold. Successive English monarchs left the policing and pillage of Wales to the Marcher Lords, and created a very real danger in the minds of Welsh princes that they were about to be conquered. The Braose, Clare and Mortimer earls were happy to maintain that territorial pressure, even though the English monarchy had no particular interest in expanding its territory. An understanding that raiding threats from Wales and Scotland were unlikely was just as worthy as forced loyalty, which no medieval monarch would have believed anyway.

Equally, we should not overlook the notion that decades and then centuries of conflict benefit populations through the survival and fortitude of their leaders—including monarchs. This hypothesis does not for one moment ignore the terror and social and physical destructive consequence of warfare. In the history of Wales in the immediate post-Norman Conquest era, the princes were seen as leaders who failed hopelessly to unite the people and put up what nineteenth-century political philosophers would term 'one nationism'. Wales at this time was anything but people of one nation. There was nothing but regional identity; but that identity was deep-rooted. Was it unlikely that princes and minor Welsh kings would be leaders of people with a sense of fierce independence and resilience—even in the gradual occupation of the south-west by Norman knights?

Leadership in its acceptance (reluctant or otherwise) of thirteenth-century English dominance would continue to exist as one of the foremost functions of monarchy—ancient or modern—and as a symbol

---

[4] Henry II, Richard I, John, Henry III.

of national identity.[5] Here was the identity of the prince as the chief-tain of 'Fair Wales', said the thirteenth-century Dafyyd Benfras, but subsequently, also according to the poet, as the ruler of rulers, meaning that his eulogy was directed at the impressive prince-administrator of Gwynedd, a territory protected by that magnificent geological redoubt, Snowdonia, and that would have troubled even the likes of Hannibal. Llywelyn ab Iorwerth (1172–1240) was called Llywelyn the Great and the sobriquet was deserved. By 1200 he had become the senior of the princes and was overlord of Pura Wallia, territories not run by the Marcher Lords. The Marcher Lords controlled Marchia Wallia. The Welsh princes had something of a respite from English raiders during the civil wars in twelfth- and thirteenth-century England, but these were brief interludes and would not put off the Edwardian conquest.

Llywelyn brought together the weaker princes and gained the recog-nition of the not very sure King John who, in return for Llywelyn's fealty and support against Scotland, went as far to approve his marriage to his step-daughter, Joan—which was just as well, because when Llywelyn fell from favour and was invaded by the English, it was the daughter who pleaded that Llywelyn should retain his dignity, his land west of the Conway and therefore his life. John never reigned under his own terms. He had almost no power other than his title of king. Two years on John fell to the powerful instincts and persuasions of his barons; by 1216, the recalcitrant Welsh princes recognised their own weakness as individuals and bowed before the great prince, who in turn helped to ease tensions with the Marcher Lords by marrying off his daughters to them.

The Saxon expediency of diplomatic marriages survived the Conquest, as it would for centuries to come. But this Welsh prince was not content to be a baronial father-in-law and royal son-in-law. He changed the authority of most of the other princes. They came to give him their allegiance because they relied on him and his undoubted authority. The princes in effect became his barons; should there be

---

[5] M. Richter, 'The Political and Institutional Background to National Consciousness in Medieval Wales', p.38, *Nationality and the Pursuit of National Independence*, T.W.Moody (ed.), Belfast, 1978.

princely capriciousness, then the one-time princes of authority would find themselves tested. Llywelyn came at a time of great state change throughout Europe. His perceptions and talents were not hidden beneath or behind any black hill of Welsh isolation. He heralded the beginning in the British Isles of that institution that the island people, as well as mainland populations, would come to scorn but would well recognise as vital to how they would now live under powerful leaders—bureaucracy.

Bureaucracy by the thirteenth century in Wales was small, sophisticated and with few real powers. Its titles and officers could be found in the English bureaucracy. Llywelyn had with him the trappings of offices in his chamberlains and treasurers, as well as stewards and justiciars, and, because of these offices, there came also the most convertible of bureaucratic currency: influence and patronage. The Welsh prince and his lords in tenancy, his princelings, had learned much from the nation beyond the Marches. Certainly the Marcher Lords were guilty, especially in the east and south, of pillaging Welsh territory and dignity. Yet there is the other aspect, too, often ignored: the relationship between the Welsh and the Marcher baronial sentries was complicated by the *Realpolitik* of the times, together with the instincts in medieval societies. Historical complexities are often simply those least understood or pondered and so the reality hampers the search for historical truth. The reality of the relationship between the Marcher and Welsh societies was that they had similar interests and even ambitions.

The Marchers may not have been absorbed into Welshness, but did they not over years assume similar regional identities with intermarriages at all levels and territorial and local custom and practice? Both understood and sometimes encouraged the idea that assimilation proved to be no difficulty in settling a potentially aggressive and abrasive crown and princely interest. The Marchers became slightly more Welsh. The Welsh princes retained their identities, but assumed greater responsibility of English affairs—which was not what the English monarchy had thought likely. Llywelyn was at Runnymede in 1215 at the signing by King John of Magna Carta. This was no social state occasion.

In Magna Carta there were three important clauses providing for the Welsh princes. These were a reminder of the importance by the opening of the thirteenth century of the power and significance of the Welsh monarchs, and, noticeably, Llywelyn was accompanied on that day by the powerful Marcher Lord, Reginald de Braose, his son-in-law. It was not always a cosy relationship, as we see when de Braose's heir, William de Braose, was found in bed with Llywelyn's wife, Princess Joan. Llywelyn hanged William.

At a political level, rather than as a local difficulty, we can further judge the importance of the great prince when the boy king, Henry III, came to power in 1216 and the crown issued a summons for Llywelyn to go to Worcester to swear loyalty to the new monarch. This was no extraordinary or diminishing act of submission. Instead, it demonstrated the authority of Llywelyn, who would be expected to have the power to bring into line any recalcitrant Welsh princeling.[6] When time came to appoint his heir, Llywelyn set aside the claims of his eldest son, Gruffydd, because he was illegitimate. Instead, Gruffydd's younger brother, Dafydd, was chosen and recognised, but only after his mother, Princess Joan, was declared to be the legitimate daughter of King John and so the approval of Pope Honorius III for the succession was obtained: a reminder of the relationship between Church and state, and of the religious base of kingship.

Four decades after he had taken power over such a large part of Wales, Llywelyn died in 1240, in the Cistercian abbey at Aberconwy he founded, robed in the religious habit he had assumed shortly after the death of his wife three years earlier. Perhaps he had not achieved all his ambitions, but the lasting significance of Llywelyn ap Gruffydd was that he established authority within his own lands and with successive English monarchs. Llywelyn 'the Great'? Probably a prince with no need for labels. Gruffydd was disgraced and he died in 1244 attempting to escape from his cell high in the Tower of London. But it was his second son by Serena ferch Rhodri who would be the last great prince of independent Wales. When Dafydd ap Llywelyn died without issue in 1246, he was succeeded by the 'new' Llywelyn ap Gruffydd who would be remembered as Llywelwyn Ein Llyw Olaf—Our Last Leader Llywelyn,

---

[6] Roderick, A.J., *The Feudal Relationship between the English Crown and the Welsh Princes*, in *History* Vol XXXVII, 1952.

Llewellyn the Great on his deathbed with his sons.
From the 11th to the 15th century the warring
Welsh princes were far more powerful than often
recorded and too often their sense of kingship is
airbrushed out of British history.

or Llywelyn the Last (1223–82). He would perish in the conquest
of Wales by Edward I. By the time of Llywelyn the Great's death in
1240, the English acknowledged his mastery of his principality, but in
effect regarded him and his princelings as a collection of barons. The
Edwardian invasion plan for 1282 was to bring the principality to heel
and spectacularly rid Wales of those who would call themselves prince
and exactly that happened. This Llywelyn had battled with the English
since the start of his reign. He had been forced to treat with the English
usurper, Simon de Montfort the Younger, with the 1267 Treaty of
Montgomery. He had forced King Henry to recognise him, battled with

Roger Mortimer and Humphrey de Bohun, and only survived an assas-
sination plot by Dafydd, his brother, because a snowstorm stopped the
plotters literally in their tracks.

He was, according to the Welsh, a great prince, but sometimes tactically inept. For example, he had stayed loyal to Simon de Montfort,
whose daughter, Eleanor de Montfort, he wanted to marry. This upset
Edward I because Eleanor was his first cousin and that would have
been at the very least constitutionally uncomfortable. They did marry
(Eleanor died in childbirth in 1282), but only after Llywelyn the Last
had been stripped of many of his privileges, land holdings, status
and the realisation that many of the Welsh princelings had come out
for Edward. They largely rescinded their unquestioning fealty to the
English monarch and the open conflict that appeared to have started
with the possibility of a truce ended at the Orewin Bridge at Builth
Wells, where Llywelyn, apparently cut off from his main forces, was
killed by an English lancer.

Edward I ordered Llywelyn's head be raised on a lance and displayed at
the Tower of London, where it remained on show for more than a decade.
As for the once-rebellious son Dafydd, he was hanged, drawn and quar-
tered at Shrewsbury. For good measure, Dafydd's two sons were thrown in
Bristol prison, never to emerge alive; the only daughter of the last prince of
independent Wales and Eleanor, Gwenllian, was taken as a baby and put in
Sempringham Priory until her death in 1337. The proud independence of
Wales had been scuffed into the dirt, and with it a realisation among Welsh
aristocracy that their titles and standing counted for little; even those who
had gone over to the English king could not for long expect reward. Most
of them with holdings became not much more than well-bred landlords.
The slights and slays festered, and it was from this stock that the rebellion
against the English crown was led in 1400 by Owain ap Gruffudd Fychan,
sometimes known as Owain Glyndŵr.

Given the importance of Welsh princes and chiefdoms in the Middle
Ages in particular, it is a puzzle why Welsh history is airbrushed from
the story of Britain. The late University of Wales history professor Alf
Williams (1925–95) was of the mind that it was the thirteenth-century
Edwardian conquest and colonisation and not the princes that made

Seal of the great Owain Glyndŵr (Owen Glendower)
c.1354–c.1416.

Wales one nation.[7] The feudal and medieval princes and monarchs created the identities of nations that we perhaps recognise in the twenty-first century. It is at this stage that we can see the pattern of the relationship between the monarchy and the people, and, therefore, the development of both. For a moment let us live with the argument that the identity of the nation (as seen by others) is the nature and constitutional reputation of the monarch incumbent. After Edward I's death in 1307, England was still in an era of Magna Carta development, almost a century after its signing, and its first issue in 1216, and its reissues in 1217 and 1225, and its confirmation in 1299, with the sixty-three clauses of the document still dominated by the promise in paragraphs thirty-nine and forty devoted to the safety and justice for all free men. The Welsh princes were part of this changing process of recognition of developing nationhood. So too were the clan leaders and princes and kings of Scotland.

[7] Williams, Professor G.A., *When Was Wales: A History of the Welsh*, p.85, Penguin, London, 1985.

CHAPTER FIVE

The Making of the Kingdom of Scotland

I n the twenty-first century it would be easy to argue that Scotland has a stronger identity than England. The territory and the sound of the language are easily branded as Scottish, whereas the longer established English nation is a diverse and not so easily identifiable society. The Venerable Bede completed his memorable, if Alfredian, *The Ecclesiastical History of the English People* in AD 731. The title tells us that the scholar of the monastery at Jarrow was familiar with the concept that in these islands there was a society called 'the English' and that they lived more or less in the state we would recognise as England. Bede's title was not 'The Ecclesiastical History of England'. In 731 there was no established England ruled by a monarch. It would be 926 before a king, Athelstan, was acknowledged King of England, the state, but the significance of these dates is the reminder that when Athelstan assumed the throne of England there had long been a recognition of the land of the English. The evidence in Scotland is that although the title King of the Scots, Rí Alban, was used in 900, there was no clear description of what constituted Scotland and who were regarded as Scots.[1] He was king neither of Wales nor of Scotland.

The question of when Scotland became Scotland can therefore be recognised as an intriguing part of the quest for Britain's medieval foundations, just as much as that of when England became England.[2] It is the norm to declare that Scots arrived from Ireland in the fifth century, settled Argyll and that within four centuries ruled over what had been the land of the Picts, roughly large swathes of modern Scotland. Yet there is little evidence that these people understood what Scotland was and who the Scots were; they regarded themselves as Irish, Gaels with an unambiguous Gaelic cultural identity and a direct racial connection with the Irish kings.

Not until the fourteenth century was there an unquestionable and defining reference to Scotland as a nation with its own people and borders, and there was reference to neither Scotland nor the Scots being Irish. On 6 April 1320, Scotland's equivalent of the eighteenth-century American Declaration of Independence, and thus the significant identity document in Scottish history, appeared as the Declaration of Arbroath.[3]

At the time of the declaration, the Scots were at war with the English in the Wars of Scottish Independence that began in 1293 when King John Balliol refused any further allegiance to Edward I of England. A series of battles and full warfare raised by Edward I's victory over the Scots at Dunbar in 1296 and Sir William Wallace's successful rebellion against Edwardian rule the following year came to nought for the English king. Incidentally, Edward I's expeditions north of his border suggest that Scotland was a recognisable state collectively defending its lands as well as borders.

A war of independence was raised again by Robert the Bruce in 1314, which led to the utter defeat of Edward II at Bannockburn. There was a truce with the Treaty of Edinburgh of 17 March 1328 and England's apparent recognition of Scottish independence under Robert I. In truth

---

[1] See Broun, Professor Dauvit, 'When did Scotland become Scotland?', *History Today*, vol. 46, 1996.

[2] *ibid.*

[3] In the USA, 6 April is officially 'Tartan Day'.

there was no peace. Edward III, who signed the Edinburgh treaty, was preoccupied with war against the French king, otherwise there would have been even greater effort by the English to retake Scotland. This conflict angered the Church because it had declared that all military might had to be concentrated on what it saw as a threat from Islam. The Scots were threatened with excommunication. The Declaration of Arbroath is a letter written to the then pope, the French cleric John XXII, in Avignon.[4] It was authored by Abbot Bernard at Arbroath Abbey and meant to be read with a similar declaration of the king, Robert the Bruce.[5] Bruce was not favoured by the pope because he had usurped the role of the previous king. The declaration amounted to a plea to the Church to understand its position in defending its right to statehood and nationhood and lift the excommunication. Whatever the reasoning behind the Declaration of Arbroath, it was the first and most important documented description of Scottish statehood, and built on the Edinburgh treaty of two years earlier. Famously, the plea to the pope was contained in one sentence that could easily have been used as a template for the American Declaration of Independence more than four hundred years later:

> as long as but a hundred of us remain alive, never will we on any conditions be brought under English rule. It is in truth not for glory, nor riches, nor honours that we are fighting, but for freedom—for that alone, which no honest man gives up but with life itself.

The pope was never going to be impressed, however plaintive the plea. The war went on. The English were never to conquer Scotland and with not a little irony it was a Scottish monarch, James VI, who, on the death of Elizabeth I in 1603, becoming James I of England, created what

---

[4] The papacy sat in Avignon between 1309 and 1376 after the election of Clement V established the open rift between Rome and the French monarchy over who should be the temporal leader of Christendom. The five popes at Avignon were all French. See Zutshi, P.N.R., 'The Avignon Papacy', *The New Cambridge Medieval History: c.1300–c.1415*, vol. VI, Jones, Michael (ed.), CUP, Cambridge, 2000.
[5] 1274–1329.

Edward III had failed to do: rule in both countries. This was a union of the crowns. The constitutional union that gave the English monarchy Scotland would not take place until the 1707 Act of Union, although Scotland would retain its legal system and its Church. It still does.

The lists of Scottish kings and queens are usually shown from the eleventh century, and here there is a similarity to English monarchy inasmuch as the Scottish kings were more tribal, clan chieftains, and not monarchs of the state of Scotland. Consequently, when Scottish monarchy was established, it became a variable feast. The tenth-century king, Cináed (or Kenneth) II, heads the list of western European princes embedded in a commentary on Old Testament history. In the next generation an Irish writer considered Cináed's son, the early eleventh-century king, Máel Coluim (or Malcolm) II, to be the glory of Europe, and a contemporary French historian praised him as a valiant warrior and a most Christian king.[6] But what of this title 'king'?

Getting to the early structure of Scottish monarchy is hindered by the lack of pre-tenth-century Scottish material. The Irish chronicles help, but the Scottish view is missing and it is not until the latter part of the eleventh century that we can find the first full conditions of monarchy; it is in the royal charter during the reign of Duncan II.[7] Furthermore, we have to tackle the system of selecting monarchy in order to crosscheck dates, and the houses of contenders and pretenders, and the realms of both. We have to think about early Scots choosing a monarch rather than accepting a simple line of succession. This procedure leaves confusion when the regular procedures cannot be followed. Take the example of accepting a leader when there were doubts about the normal male line. The Picts simply picked a monarch from the female line, instead of the regular pool of males following the precedent of the early Welsh,

---

[6] Hudson, Benjamin T., *Kings of Celtic Scotland*, p.xi (Contributions to the Study of World History 43), Greenwood Press, Westport, Connecticut, 1994.

[7] The difficulties of useful discussion are emphasised by lack of corroborative text. For example, the limited number of texts makes it hard to crosscheck even something as basic as titles and dates. Something as important as the chronicle of John of Fordun, which is dated from the late part of the fourteenth century, has to stand alone as a source even when trying to balance it with the writings in *Liber Pluscardensis*, the Scottish history up to 1603 written in Pluscarden Priory, Elgin.

who had accepted the order of possession was decided by order of preference—social status and caste ruled as they had famously when the English king, Athelstan, had to fight off claims to the throne by those who said he had no right to be king because his mother was a concubine rather than a wife.

The missing link in understanding the early Scottish monarchy is the lack of a proper bureaucracy. Bureaucracy's single redeeming feature is that it is, and was from the beginning, full of jobsworths. The best, even the earliest, jobsworths were pedants. The instinct of the pedant is justification, often self-justification, and that means a collection of regulation and precedence, and so, for the researcher-cum-historian, written record. This is where the problem for proper interpretation of Scottish royal history lies: it was not until the twelfth century that there was royal government and therefore fewer sources of record. When the change came it did so under the influence of the long-established English system of officialdom, from chamberlain to steward of the greater households to the regional and area baileys and sheriffs.

The Norman Conquest began in 1066 and this was the period of the transition from the royal working structures of the Saxons to the advanced systems put in place with the spread of accountable Norman communities. By the time of the regions of sheriffs, the bureaucracies were providing detailed records of the life and expansion of Scotland under kings; these kings understood the advantages of establishing, maintaining and recording the workings of a judiciary by the mid- to late thirteenth century. Moreover, the precedent of such record keeping came from the long-established English system of bureaucracy whereby educated clerks and clerics kept faithful records of the goings on in lower orders as well as within the emerging aristocracy.

By the thirteenth century there was a joining of the development role of the ecclesiastical scribes and record keepers, though this was nothing as widespread and complete as the much larger English bureaucracy and the acceptance of succession by precedence. The record that the king's eldest son or the eldest male issue of that son would inherit the throne was intact. There was no question of a female line; nor was there a body that could examine the credentials of the successor. A monarch could leave the crown to his eldest boy even if he was something of a nincompoop and clearly a man or child of doubtful authority.

This was the case in 1205, when the Earl of Huntingdon had to give way to the precedence of the child Alexander, the son of William I. The earl's initial reluctance was considered divisive, in the sense that it caused a schism, as any rivalry might. This regularisation of the protocols of Scottish monarchy that had not truly existed in the previous century was coincidental in the thirteenth century with bringing under the monarchy the allegiance of greater parts of Scotland, by the nineteenth century generally referred to as the Highlands and Islands. From this, monarchy could better bring administrative stability necessary for the growing state as well as, for example, adventures and incursions across its own state and national borders into northern England; it did so in the name of a Scottish monarchy that could be followed, and it could thus add to the historical identity of monarchy and people. After all, it is not until Alexander II (1214–49) that we find references to the area south of the River Forth and the Firth of Clyde as part of 'Scotland'.[8] The later chronicles gathered information and interpretation; for example, we learn more of family and estate history from the 1251 and 1317 *Chronicles of the Picts and Scots,* which have details quite omitted from earlier texts, including the all-important list of regal relatives and birth and places of death. This is essential picture-building material, but data to be used with a warning: how do we know it is true?

The easy assumption about the earliest kings is that there was no established principle of primogeniture, even though there is evidence that the tenth-century Kenneth II wished the nearest blood survivor to succeed. There is no evidence, however, that Kenneth was mighty enough to have his wish recognised. It was still the case that the strongest sword remained the surest badge of the crown office.

We might also think about the manner of succession. There was no formal or religious crowning of the king. Again, information is not yet come by, but the chronicle of John of Fordun in 1249 tells us that Alexander III was neither anointed nor crowned, but inaugurated by the cemetery cross in the yard of the church of Scone. For simplicity in this discussion on the future of monarchy and the importance of the past (how else do we judge our identity fully?), it is as well to split

---

[8] Broun, Professor Dauvit, *op.cit.*

the Scottish kings into six houses: the MacAlpins, Morays, Dunkelds, Balliols, Bruces and Stewarts—who became, after the death of Mary Queen of Scots in 1567, the Stuarts under the then one-year-old James VI. The MacAlpins were prominent in the Dark Ages of Scotland, a land of the aboriginal Picts in the north-east, descendants of the continental European Celts; of the northern Irish Gaelic Celts—the Gaels—who saw themselves as 'good family' Irish who had arrived in the third and fourth centuries, and who lived in Dalriada, the West Highlands; of the Britons in the south-west; of the Vikings of Denmark and Norway in the Shetlands and Orkney; and of the Angles (the English) from Northumbrian lands who settled the borders.

Into this brose of proud and warring peoples, Cináed mac Alpín—in modern script, Kenneth I MacAlpin—was born on the island of Iona in AD 810. Benjamin Hudson's *Kings of Celtic Scotland* demonstrates the difficulties of pinning down an accurate history of the creation of the first king of the Scots.[9] Before the ninth century, what we would later call Scotland we should best describe as a series of geographical territories. Kenneth MacAlpin was not the first tribal king to attempt to bring the territorial factions into one realm. Many of the ancestors of MacAlpin and his like came from what is now County Antrim, on the north-east coastal corner of Northern Ireland. This was the Irish kingdom of Dál Riata, mostly a huddle of the seemingly insignificant refugees from Munster. Although evidence is hard to come by, a remarkably detailed, early eighth-century tax and muster role found in *Senchus Fer nAlban*, an Irish history of the men of Scotland, is the earliest census recorded in Britain. The first version of *Senchus Fer nAlban* was finished in the seventh century[10] (Domesday is not until the eleventh century). Some of the conclusions and claims in and for this document may be set aside. What is not in doubt is that this census of military and tax-paying obligations of the people suggests that Dalriada had the most advanced structure of government anywhere in the islands of Britain

---

[9] Hudson, Benjamin T., *op.cit.* See also Anderson, O.M., *Kings and Kingship in Early Scotland* (2011) and Bannerman, John, *Studies in the History of Dalriada* (1974).

[10] It is in the library of Trinity College, Dublin.

at the time. Importantly for our story, the *Senchus Fer nAlban* gives us genealogies of Scottish nobility as well as census figures.

We date Kenneth MacAlpin from the ninth century and his importance is as the king who unified the five mini-nations or peoples: the Picts of the Forth and Clyde, the Angles of Lothian, to some extent the Norse from the islands as well as the far north in Sutherland and Caithness, the (former Irish) Scots in Argyll, and the descendants of northern Britons from England. With an achievement such as Kenneth's, we might hope for a written, albeit exaggerated, record of these times. It was not a time for accurate record and if some did survive outside the monasteries none have been found.

We can claim Kenneth I, however, as the first of the so-called early kings. His name MacAlpin comes from *mac* ('son of') and Alpin (his father's name). No early king of Scotland was much different from his southern counterpart inasmuch as he held and gained territory by his sword's strength rather than diplomacy or personality. Kenneth is recorded as the fierce warrior who protected his small kingdom by attacking the Strathclyde Britons, and leading raiding parties as well as skirmishes into the higher latitude of Northumbria. The seemingly constant battles were often very small-scale affairs, but enough blood was let and anxiety heated for both sides to see the sense in a truce, if not peace.

To help the one and hope for the other, Kenneth, in the time's custom, married his daughter to Rhun, King of the Britons in Strathclyde. His triumph that gave him the throne came in AD 843, when defeating the Picts he brought the two groups of families, or clans, together to form the Kingdom of Alba. The rest followed and by his death (from severe illness, perhaps, rather than any wound) in 858, Kenneth was properly king and had established an understanding of what survives into the twenty-first century, namely kingship. Kingship was and remains a mood and temper of loyalty whereby allegiance is a two-way affair: protection of a king's people in return for their loyalty. This was and remains an uncertain agreement between leader and led; yet it is the basis of family. In Kenneth and his Saxon equivalents it was the principle that established identity. Donald I (858–62) and Constantine I (862–77) were sons of Kenneth and little record survives about them, other than that Constantine was killed and allegedly beheaded during

Victorian production of Macbeth in accurate period dress,
starring Charles Keen in 1848. 'The Scottish Play' was not
altogether historically accurate.

a battle with the Norse at Forgan, Fife. His sibling, Aed, who lived by his Gaelic name, 'fire', survived for a year and was killed by the next king, Giric; then Donald II struggled with invaders for a decade and the throne was a scrappy affair, with little authority, until the arrival of Constantine II in 900. He was to reign for an extraordinary period of forty-three years.

It was this reign that ended with the coincidence of one of the most historically important English monarchs, the Wessex Anglo-Saxon king, Athelstan. Constantine, a son of Aed, would appear to have spent much of his remarkably long reign—four decades—fighting and treating with invaders during Norse raids from Ireland (he married one daughter to Olaf III in the hope of blood loyalty), and raided the northern boundaries of England to defeat the ambitions of Britons and Saxons. It came to nothing in AD 937, when the final heave of Athelstan's determination to rule not just the English people, but also the land of England, met the final resistance of the Scots at Brunanburh. This battle decided the future authority of the English throughout the British Isles and established an authority across continental Europe that was to survive, albeit with dramatic ebbs and flows, for more than a thousand years.

Of the thirteen Scottish monarchs who followed Constantine, none is much remembered outside Scotland other than Duncan, killed by Macbeth. Duncan was the son of the lay Abbot of Dunkeld and Malcolm II's daughter, Bethoc (from the Gaelic for 'life' or 'bringer of life'), and took the throne from his grandfather, Malcolm, in 1034. He was neither popular (perhaps too English in his ways) nor successful. Duncan was lucky to survive the skirmishes and battles of his misfortune until one of his commanders, the character better known as Shakespeare's Macbeth, killed him in a battle by Elgin, in Morayshire, in August 1040. Macbeth, the son of a high steward, perhaps the Earl of Moray, was to rule for fifteen years. The difference between the Shakespearean image here is obvious. The Bard has the Macbeths plotting the murder of and killing an ancient Duncan when he visits them, but in truth he killed him in battle when Duncan was thirty-eight.

The origins of Scottish royalty did not culminate with the cult of Bonnie Prince Charlie but with James VI. He was the last of the great Scottish monarchs whose belief in the divine right to rule, or at least his own God-given right, was intellectually argued more successfully than his predecessors had tried with targe and claymore. When in 1603 James VI of Scotland became James I of England, the ambitions of Elizabeth's privy councillor Robert Cecil, who had nursed the succession from Tudor to Stuart, should have borne fruit. The political, diplomatic and religious apples of seventeenth-century British monarchy were sour. It should have been so different.

This simple example of the development of Scottish monarchy, state and people is more than a bit of history punctuated by dates and kings, and skirmishes and power changes. It is an important aspect of inherited identity for Scots, whose monarch abandoned them in 1603 for the prize of the English throne and the doubtful claim that this was the time for a union of two crowns; although in constitutional form, it was exactly that: James VI saw that Scotland and England should be unified for military and even economic reasons and that was far more than the symbolism of being king of both countries. This made some sense constitutionally, but it threatened identity and no monarch might be allowed to do that. Identity was more important to the Scots than to the English. A constant area of difference between the two nations has been the divisions of Christian worship, so much so that Charles I's determination to press his common liturgy on the Scottish Church, the Kirk, led indirectly to the English Civil War, the king's execution and Puritan rule in England for a decade during the mid-seventeenth century. The open conflict is pertinent to our story because of the constitutional entwinement of the British monarch, the state Church and Parliament.

CHAPTER SIX

The Middle Monarchs and the Making of the Anglican Church

T he British monarch is supreme governor of the Church of England. The governorship is a solemn duty and, depending on the monarch, taken with a seriousness that has ranged from the authority to defy papal usurpation to fear of foreign invasion by Catholic monarchies or societies, mostly France and Spain. The authority that goes with the title is contained in the document known as the *Thirty-Nine Articles*, the unequivocal statement of Church of England doctrine. Their origin is in the forty-two of them set down in 1552 by Thomas Cranmer,[1] an architect of what became known as the English Reformation. They, in turn, had their origins in thirteen articles contained in an ambitious agreement between Henry VIII and the seven Lutheran princes in 1536 that the English church shied from. The different versions of articles had in earlier versions one significant theme represented neatly in the Lutheran *Augsburg Confession* of 1530: the articles 'dissent in no article of faith from the Catholic Church'.

The importance of this sentiment would have been quite obvious

---

[1] 1489–1556.

in the sixteenth century. Even Henry VIII's dissent from Rome did not radically alter the liturgy and beliefs. Christianity in whichever persuasion did not reject the Trinity; the rejections were in the form of the liturgical content and for the English Church, the rejection of the authority of Rome over what Henry VIII called his empire—meaning, Britain. Hence the importance that the *Thirty-Nine Articles* remained the Church of England's declaration of doctrine rather than belief. Of course, it is doctrine that reflects the emphasis of belief and so the monarch's role was of paramount importance during a time when law was the express wish and could so often reflect the capriciousness of the sovereign.

The articles are a companion to the solemn authority of the Book of Common Prayer and so tells a worshipper in the Church of England exactly what she or he is expected to believe and how liturgically to express that belief publicly or in private. For our purpose, above all of the beliefs and gestures is Article Thirty-Seven as described in the 1571 and 1662 texts:

> The King's Majesty hath the chief power in this Realm of England, and other his Dominions, unto whom the chief Government of all Estates of this Realm, whether they be Ecclesiastical or Civil, in all causes doth appertain, and is not, nor ought to be, subject to any foreign Jurisdiction. Where we attribute to the King's Majesty the chief government, by which Titles we understand the minds of some slanderous folks to be offended; we give not our Princes the ministering either of God's Word, or of the Sacraments, the which thing the Injunctions also lately set forth by Elizabeth our Queen do most plainly testify; but that only prerogative, which we see to have been given always to all godly Princes in holy Scriptures by God himself; that is, that they should rule all estates and degrees committed to their charge by God, whether they be Ecclesiastical or Temporal, and restrain with the civil sword the stubborn and evil-doers.
>
> The Bishop of Rome hath no jurisdiction in this Realm of England.
>
> The Laws of the Realm may punish Christian men with death, for heinous and grievous offences.

Act of Supremacy 1534, which established Henry VIII as supreme head or governor of the Church of England.

There we have the historical authority of the monarch as supreme governor of the state Church. The true power is nothing more than to carry out duties rather than to insist on the consequences of those duties. As an example of this, the monarch is expected to approve the appointment of senior clerical members of the Church of England. As the monarch has no power of veto, royal consent is a formal acceptance of advice. Yet the fact that the monarch remains invested as head of the state Church, even in this form, immediately raises a three-part question: first, is there a case for the Church of England remaining a state Church—can it stay a state Church without the monarch being at its head; second, should it be disestablished; third, would disestablishment usurp the monarch's greater role?

The immediate answer to the third part may be summed up in this fashion: the monarch's supreme power is that of public symbolism. In the modern century the monarch has few powers other than ceremonial or quirky ones: that would describe the monarch's position in the Church, were it not for royal symbolism in the British psyche even when, as in this case, there is little evidence that the British people are aware that the monarch holds this title and position.

The 1534 Act of Supremacy established Henry VIII as head of the Church and the ruling nobility's recognition of his authority. In theory, therefore, the monarch's position would meet with universal approval. The 1534 Act left little to chance or ambiguity:

> Albeit the king's Majesty justly and rightfully is and ought to be the supreme head of the Church of England, and so is recognized by the clergy of this realm in their convocations, yet nevertheless, for corroboration and confirmation thereof, and for increase of virtue in Christ's religion within this realm of England, and to repress and extirpate all errors, heresies, and other enormities and abuses heretofore used in the same, be it enacted, by authority of this present Parliament, that the king, our sovereign lord, his heirs and successors, kings of this realm, shall be taken, accepted, and reputed the only supreme head in earth of the Church of England, called Anglicans Ecclesia; and shall have and enjoy, annexed and united to the imperial crown of this realm, as well the title and style thereof, as all honors, dignities, preeminences, jurisdictions, privileges, authorities, immunities, profits, and commodities to the said dignity of the supreme head of the same Church belonging and appertaining; and that our said sovereign lord, his heirs and successors, kings of this realm, shall have full power and authority from time to time to visit, repress, redress, record, order, correct, restrain, and amend all such errors, heresies, abuses, offenses, contempts and enormities, whatsoever they be, which by any manner of spiritual authority or jurisdiction ought or may lawfully be reformed, repressed, ordered, redressed, corrected, restrained, or amended, most to the pleasure of Almighty God, the increase of virtue in Christ's religion, and for the conservation of the peace, unity, and tranquility of this realm; any usage, foreign land, foreign authority, prescription, or any other thing or things to the contrary hereof notwithstanding.

There were two Acts of Supremacy, the first as above in 1534 and the second in 1559. As the single title suggests, the Acts served a double purpose: to remove the pope as head of the English Church, in which Henry was probably correct if he thought the Church in England (as opposed to the later Church of England) had little theological integrity;

and to establish the British monarch in his place as head of the English Church. The common belief remains that Henry usurped the pope's authority simply to bring about his divorce from Catherine of Aragon.[2] That is part of the story. We should remember more broadly the movement that was to become the European Reformation and the awareness, certainly by Henry, who was a theological scholar, that Pope Leo X in 1521 declared the English monarch 'Fidei Defensor' in recognition of Henry's views of Martin Luther, whom they both thought a heretic. Henry had moved on, but Rome could not; thus the rebellion against total acceptance of the liturgical and religious authority of Rome can be seen as the beginnings of the English Reformation.

Henry's view of Luther would not change, but his annoyance with Rome, when an annulment was refused partly by the fear of the pope who was virtually the prisoner of Catherine's nephew, Emperor Charles V, was one of the consequences of the taking of Rome by the Emperor in the spring of 1527. The refusal of Pope Clement VII to annul the marriage was, as now we see it, inevitable. Not for the last time, the British would break with Rome.

It is true that the common grounds for this breach have been considered to be the politics of Henry VIII's ambition for a male heir,[3] his near obsession and personal delight at the vision of Anne Boleyn (the sister of his mistress Mary Boleyn), and a very strong belief that Rome should not have sway over Henry's British empire—the British Isles. The Roman Catholic persuasion would henceforth be outside the law. The 1534 Act of Supremacy was unambiguous: support for the Church of Rome either from religious belief or by constitutional principle was in effect an act against the authority of the monarch and therefore a treasonable act. Yet even the threat of capital punishment for such treason did not mean that the country immediately discarded its beliefs in the teachings of Rome. In 1553, Henry and Catherine of Aragon's daughter

---

[2] 1485–1536. She was queen consort to Henry VIII and, as one-time Spanish ambassador, the first European female ambassador in history.

[3] Catherine of Aragon was six times pregnant by Henry VIII, which led to three boys but only one of the six offspring survived: Mary (1516–58), to become Mary I—Bloody Mary—after the death of her half-brother, Edward VI, son of Henry and Jane Seymour.

Mary succeeded Edward VI as monarch, having swept aside the sad figure of Lady Jane Grey,[4] a devout Protestant and the granddaughter of Henry VIII's younger sister, Mary. Grey was married (evidence suggests against her will) to Guildford Dudley, the fourth son of the Earl of Northumberland, who in doomed sixteenth-century power gaming persuaded Edward to name Grey as his successor. So it was that Lady Jane Grey was proclaimed queen on 9 July 1553. According to an undertaker by the name of Henry Machyn, her 'coronation' was a hurried affair in the Tower of London:

> On 9 July all the head officers and the guard were sworn to Queen Jane as queen of England...The following day queen Jane was received into the Tower with a great company of lords and nobles ... after the queen, and the duchess of Suffolk her mother, bearing her train, with many ladies, and there was a firing of guns and chamber such as has not often been seen, between 4 and 5 o'clock; by 6 o'clock began the proclamation on the same afternoon of Queen Jane, with two heralds and a trumpet blowing, declaring that Lady Mary was unlawfully begotten, and so went through Cheapside to Fleet Street, proclaiming Queen Jane.

In not much more than a week, Mary arrived in London to claim her throne. Lady Jane Grey was spared, but not for long. In January 1554 Sir Thomas Wyatt led some three thousand men of Kent in protest against the announcement that Mary would marry the Catholic Philip of Spain. Wyatt wanted to replace Mary with the young and Protestant Elizabeth. Mary would have none of it and although not as famous as Elizabeth I's Armada's Eve 'we see the sails of the enemy' speech in 1588, her rallying cry to the faithful at Chatham was delivered with equal determination and demi-god imagery:

> I am your Queen, to whom at my coronation, when I was wedded to the realm and laws of the same (the spousal ring whereof I have on my finger, which never hitherto was, not [sic] hereafter

---

[4] 1537–54.

shall be, left off), you promised your allegiance and obedience to me.... And I say to you, on the word of a Prince, I cannot tell how naturally the mother loveth the child, for I was never the mother of any; but certainly, if a Prince and Governor may as naturally and earnestly love her subjects as the mother doth love the child, then assure yourselves that I, being your lady and mistress, do as earnestly and tenderly love and favour you. And I, thus loving you, cannot but think that ye as heartily and faithfully love me; and then I doubt not but we shall give these rebels a short and speedy overthrow.[5]

Short and speedy indeed was the sum of the rebels' defeat. Wyatt and many of his men were dispatched to await the axeman's pleasure. If the rebellion was truly raised to foil the arrangement of two Catholic houses—Mary I and Philip II—then Mary could no longer imagine herself in charity with her Protestant kinswoman. Grey and Dudley were sent to the block in February 1554. The manner of execution could be softened neither by the dignity of the victims nor the imagined right cause of the condemnation. Here, though, we have over 450 years ago the very example of the monarch's unquestioned power and the purpose of that power: to execute not just perpetrators but cause.

His [Guildford's] carcase thrown into a cart, and his head in a cloth, he was brought to the chapel within the Tower, where the Lady Jane, whose lodging was in Partidge's house, did see his dead carcase taken out of the cart, as well as she did see him before alive on going to his death—a sight to her no less than death. By this time was there a scaffold made upon the green over against the White Tower, for the said Lady Jane to die upon.... The said lady, being nothing abashed....with a book in her hand whereon she prayed all the way till she came to the said scaffold.... First, when she mounted the said scaffold she said to the people standing thereabout: 'Good people, I am come hither to die, and

[5] Foxe, John (1518–87), *The Actes and Monuments of these latter and perillous days*, long known as Foxe's *Book of Martyrs*.

by a law I am condemned to the same. The fact, indeed, against
the queen's highness was unlawful, and the consenting there-
unto by me: but touching the procurement and desire thereof by
me or on my behalf, I do wash my hands thereof in innocency,
before God, and the face of you, good Christian people, this day'
and therewith she wrung her hands, in which she had her book.
And then, kneeling down, she turned to Feckenham [the dean of
St Paul's] saying, 'Shall I say this psalm?' And he said, 'Yea.' Then
she said the psalm of *Miserere mei Deus*, in English, in most devout
manner, to the end. Then she stood up and gave...Mistress Tilney
her gloves and handkercher, and her book to master Bruges,
the lieutenant's brother; forthwith she untied her gown. The
hangman went to her to help her therewith; then she desired him
to let her alone, and also with her other attire and neckercher,
giving to her a fair handkercher to knit about her eyes. Then the
hangman kneeled down, and asked her forgiveness, whom she
gave most willingly.

Then he willed her to stand upon the straw: which doing, she
saw the block. Then she said, 'I pray you dispatch me quickly.'
Then she kneeled down, saying, 'Will you take it off before I lay
me down?' and the hangman answered her, 'No, madame.' She
tied the kercher about her eyes; then feeling for the block said,
'What shall I do? Where is it?' One of the standers-by guiding her
thereto, she laid her head down upon the block, and stretched
forth her body and said: 'Lord, into thy hands I commend my
spirit!' And so she ended.[6]

Mary had embarked on her crusade to restore the unfettered Catholic
faith in her realm and therefore to disestablish the Church of England,
an act not repeated until Oliver Cromwell and the Commonwealth a
hundred years later. Constitutional and religious events during this
period of English history are perhaps too easily described as contro-
versial; yet the basic issue—Catholic or Protestant England?—touched
the daily lives of all England. This certainly does not suggest that these

---

[6] Account by an anonymous witness.

islands were bathed in Christianity. There is no record of a devout people in any of the regions of the British Isles. Few worshipped in a sense of the doctrine of Christian Trinity being understood (this is probably the case even in the twenty-first century). Indeed, until the nineteenth-century appearance of major cities and therefore ethnic groupings, worship might have easily been witnessed as a near-filial duty to laird, lord or squire. The true religious belief of the majority of the British leaned to an easier acceptance of that which could be sensed and believed in fright and comfort in equal measure; in other words, superstition. Moreover, the Church and its priests preserved the mystery of liturgical expression and few had access to sacred texts. There was certainly discussion of the essential understanding of, say, the *mysterion*, the Pauline religious secret of the hidden purpose or counsel of God. Even the priests, often ill-educated, had little under-standing of such passions and knew little how to express what they did know.

Without any thoughts of why and which religious persuasion was to be accepted, two concepts were understood by parishioners and priests. First, Catholicism represented a long-feared threat of inva-sion from France or Spain or both and such an assault could be given papal blessing as a crusade. Second, however a man leant in his reli-gious instincts, he was to know that the monarch insisted on obedience to the Church of Rome and disobedience could mean execution. This was the position of the monarch's power vis-à-vis the Church and its people. The monarch could and did decide which church would be the state Church, and therefore which persuasions were outside the law, and how a common man might worship and where. In fact, the common man presented few difficulties for the head of the Church here on earth. The stronger feelings and even rebellion would almost certainly come from the greater families with learning and religious commitments, and this has remained so until now. Indeed, this image and awareness of the monarch's hierarchical status within the established Church would be understood in the twenty-first century partly because of the aura surrounding the monarchy, suggesting that the Queen 'owns' the nation and is in the ascendancy over all subjects, including her minis-ters and high personages.

Such authority was never more obvious than in the reign of
Mary I. Her short-lived authority over people and religion was seen as
her personal crusade to restore her role as a monarch divinely anointed.
John Foxe sets out as a preface to one of his long Church-history chap-
ters an unambiguous statement of the queen's purpose:

> For as much we are come now to the time of Queen Mary,
> when so many were put to death for the cause especially of the
> Mass, and The Sacrament of the Altar (as they call it), I
> thought it convenient, upon the occasion given, in the ingress
> of this foresaid story, first, to prefix before, by the way of
> preface, some declaration collected out of divers writers and
> authors, whereby to set forth to the reader the great absurdity,
> wicked abuse, and perilous idolatry, of the popish mass;
> declaring how, and by whom, it came in, and how it is clouted
> and patched up of divers additions: to the intent that the reader,
> seeing the vain institution thereof, and weighing the true causes
> why it is to be exploded out of all churches, may the better thereby
> judge of their death, which gave their lives for the testimony and
> the word of truth.[7]

Within such a slim calendar of events it was a Marian task that
Henry VIII's Act of Supremacy had to be repealed that very year,
1554. On 25 July, the Roman Catholic union of England and Spain
was declared when Mary I married Philip II at Winchester. Parliament
was immediately summoned by writ and, once answered, repealed the
1534 Act. The Catholic mass was restored and the notion of celibacy
proclaimed—married priests were expected to return to bachelorhood.
A practising and declaiming Protestant was now, in the eyes of English
law inspired by the monarch, a heretic and therefore more than a religious outlaw, but an enemy of the state. The block was not enough to
cleanse the heresy; in three years it is generally accepted that some
three hundred Protestants were burned at the stake.

[7] Foxe, John, *op.cit.*

The burning at the stake of Bishop Nicholas Ridley and Bishop
Hugh Latimer in 1555 for their heresy against the Catholic rule
of Queen Mary.

At distance, the tortures and executions sometimes take on a less
dreadful picture than the reality of the events. These were public executions with every agony exposed by victims who had never killed, stolen
nor defrauded a single soul. John Foxe's description in his *Actes and
Monuments* of the burning of two martyrs (for they were just that) is a
telling account of the uncompromising moment of death for religious
persuasion in the mid-sixteenth century under Queen Mary. The two to
die: the Bishop of London Nicholas Ridley (1500-55) and Hugh Latimer
(1487-1555), sometime chaplain to King Edward VI.

> Dr. Ridley, the night before execution, was very facetious,
> had himself shaved, and called his supper a marriage feast;
> he remarked upon seeing Mrs. Irish (the keeper's wife) weep,
> "though my breakfast will be somewhat sharp, my supper will be
> more pleasant and sweet." The place of death was on the north

side of the town opposite Baliol College: Dr. Ridley was dressed in a black gown furred, and Mr. Latimer had a long shroud on, hanging down to his feet. Dr. Ridley, as he passed Bocardo, looked up to see Dr. Cranmer, but the latter was then engaged in disputation with a friar.

When they came to the stake, Dr. Ridley embraced Latimer fervently, and bid him be of good heart. He then knelt by the stake, and after earnestly praying together, they had a short private conversation. Dr. Smith then preached a short sermon against the martyrs, who would have answered him, but were prevented by Dr. Marshal, the vice-chancellor. Dr. Ridley then took off his gown and tippet, and gave them to his brother-in-law, Mr. Shipside. He gave away also many trifles to his weeping friends, and the populace were anxious to get even a fragment of his garments. Mr. Latimer gave nothing, and from the poverty of his garb, was soon stripped to his shroud, and stood venerable and erect, fearless of death.

Dr. Ridley being unclothed to his shirt, the smith placed an iron chain about their waists, and Dr. Ridley bid him fasten it securely; his brother having tied a bag of gunpowder about his neck, gave some also to Mr. Latimer. Dr. Ridley then requested of Lord Williams, of Fame, to advocate with the queen the cause of some poor men to whom he had, when bishop, granted leases, but which the present bishop refused to confirm. A lighted fagot was now laid at Dr. Ridley's feet, which caused Mr. Latimer to say, "Be of good cheer, Ridley; and play the man. We shall this day, by God's grace, light up such a candle in England, as, I trust, will never be put out."

When Dr. Ridley saw the flame approaching him, he exclaimed, "Into thy hands, O Lord, I commend my spirit!" and repeated often, "Lord receive my spirit!" Mr. Latimer, too, ceased not to say, "O Father of heaven receive my soul!"

Embracing the flame, he bathed his hands in it, and soon died, apparently with little pain; but Dr. Ridley, by the ill-adjustment of the fagots, which were green, and placed too high above the furze was burnt much downwards. At this time, piteously entreating for more fire to come to him, his brother-in-law imprudently heaped the fagots up over him, which caused the fire more fiercely to burn his limbs, whence he literally leaped up and down under the fagots, exclaiming that he could not burn; indeed, his dreadful extremity was but too plain, for after his legs were quite consumed, he showed his body and shirt unsinged by the flame.

Crying upon God for mercy, a man with a bill pulled the fagots down, and when the flames arose, he bent himself towards that side; at length the gunpowder was ignited, and then he ceased to move, burning on the other side, and falling down at Mr. Latimer's feet over the chain that had hitherto supported him. Every eye shed tears at the afflicting sight of these sufferers, who were among the most distinguished persons of their time in dignity, piety, and public estimation. They suffered October 16, 1555.

Within five years, all would be recast as Henry VIII intended. Elizabeth[8] became Queen of England and Ireland in 1558.

Elizabeth was the daughter of Henry VIII and Anne Boleyn. There were two male influences in her life: her secretary and closest adviser, Sir William Cecil; and as a child her tutor in rhetoric and grammar, the Saint John's College, Cambridge scholar, Roger Ascham. On becoming queen, he joined her Court and her thinking. Ascham was as fervent a Protestant as Queen Mary was a Catholic. Ascham was a product of Reformation apocalypse theory, fearing Catholic demonism, witchcraft and soul possession.[9] He saw the Church of England as the starting point of English philosophy and thus considered that the Church of Rome had no place in the theological instruction of the people. Catholicism was not simply to be avoided; it was to be condemned as being at the very least sinister and dangerous: the 'papistrie and hewresie' of Catholicism were beyond dispute, and the Church of England must be 'Christes trewe Religion'.[10]

[8] 1533–1603.
[9] See Ascham's *The Scholemaster* of 1570 and *Toxophillius* of 1545 (more than a book about archery; *Toxophillius* sets a standard of rhetoric in the Protestant Reformation).
[10] See Stark, Ryan J., in *Journal of the History of Ideas*, pp.517–32, vol.69, no.4, October 2008.

The doubts, confrontations and religious suspicions would not escape this woman who now assumed the role of supreme governor of the state Church. It was a curious beast. The Church of her England was surely Protestant, yet its liturgy and even its clerical garb were Catholic. She was inclined to the formality of the Catholic persuasion and not so fond of the raw liturgical demands of the devoted Protestants, with their inklings of Lutherism and Scottish piety.

To test the importance of what followed on Elizabeth's accession to the throne and its consequences for the twenty-first century debate on the disestablishment of the Church of England, it is useful to look, in modern transliteration, at her Act of Supremacy, enacted with some urgency and enforced within a year of her becoming queen. It is an Act that travels far beyond theological and liturgical differences with Rome. It is a document that reveals and for centuries would continue to reveal English, even British, fears that the islands would be vulnerable to invasion—and that some invasion could be supported by powerful aristocratic factions within the British Isles. It reveals that parliamentary authority for an established Church would not by itself safeguard the boundaries and lands of the Elizabethans, nor the succeeding Stuarts' and Hanoverians'. Immediately we have quite a different origin of the role of the monarch as supreme governor of the Church of England. The opening phrases of Elizabeth's 1559 Act of Supremacy are unequivocal in the monarch's belief that what might be done in Rome's name was the true threat to the future of her people:

> An act restoring to the crown the ancient jurisdiction over the state ecclesiastical and spiritual and abolishing all foreign power repugnant to the same... may it therefore please your highness, for the repressing of the said usurped foreign power and the restoring of the rights jurisdictions, and pre-eminences appertaining to the imperial crown of this your realm, that it may be enacted by the authority of this present parliament that the said act . . . and all and every branch, clauses, and articles therein contained, other than such branches, clauses, and sentences as hereafter shall be excepted, may from the last day of this session of parliament, by authority of this present parliament, be

repealed, and shall from thenceforth be utterly void and of none effect . . .

And to the intent that all usurped and foreign power and authority, spiritual and temporal, may forever be clearly extinguished and never to be used nor obeyed within this realm or any other your majesty's countries, may it please your highness that it may be further enacted by the authority aforesaid that no foreign prince, person, prelate, state, or potentate, spiritual or temporal, shall at any time after the last day of this session of Parliament use, enjoy, or exercise any manner of power, jurisdiction, superiority, authority, pre-eminence, or privilege, spiritual or ecclesiastical, within this realm or within any other your majesty's dominions or countries that now be or hereafter shall be, but from thenceforth the same shall be clearly abolished out of this realm ... and that your highness, your heirs, and successors, kings or queens of this realm, shall have full power ... to exercise . . . all manner of jurisdictions, privileges, and pre-eminences in any wise touching or concerning any spiritual or ecclesiastical jurisdiction within these your realms. . .

An Act had no power unless a person of civic or religious authority had words in common to swear recognition of the queen's authority and their obedience:

And for the better observation and maintenance of this act, may it please your highness that it may be further enacted by the authority aforesaid that all and every archbishop, bishop, and all and every other ecclesiastical person and other ecclesiastical officer and minister, of what estate, dignity, pre-eminence, or degree soever he or they be or shall be, and all and every temporal judge, justicer, mayor, and other lay or temporal officer and minister, and every other person having your highness's fee or wages within this realm or any your highness's dominions shall make, take, and receive a corporal oath upon the Evangelist, before such person or persons as shall please your highness, your heirs or successors, under the great seal of England to assign and name to accept and take the same, according to the tenor and effect hereafter following, that is to say—

'I, ... do utterly testify and declare in my conscience that the queen's highness is the only supreme governor of this realm and of all other her highness's dominions and countries, as well in all spiritual or ecclesiastical things or causes as temporal, and that no foreign prince, person, prelate, state, or potentate hath or ought to have any jurisdiction, power, superiority, pre-eminence, or authority, ecclesiastical or spiritual, within this realm; and therefore I do utterly renounce and forsake all foreign jurisdictions, powers, superiorities, and authorities, and do promise that from henceforth I shall bear faith and true allegiance to the queen's highness, her heirs, and lawful successors, and to my power shall assist and defend all jurisdictions, pre-eminences, privileges, and authorities granted or belonging to the queen's highness, her heirs, and successors, or united or annexed to the imperial crown of this realm: so help me God and by the contents of this Book.'

And what would happen if the sentiment and verity of the oath were overlooked? Nothing was left to interpretation:

... if any person or persons dwelling or inhabiting within this your realm ... shall by writing, printing, teaching, preaching, express words, deeds, or act, advisedly, maliciously, and directly affirm, hold, stand with, set forth, maintain, or defend the authority, pre-eminence, power, or jurisdiction, spiritual or ecclesiastical, of any foreign prince, prelate, person, state, or potentate whatsoever, heretofore claimed, used, or usurped within this realm or any dominion or country being within or under the power, dominion, or obeisance of your highness, or shall advisedly, maliciously, or directly ... execute anything for the extolling, advancement, setting forth, maintenance, or defence of any such pretended or usurped jurisdiction, power, pre-eminence, or authority, or any part thereof, that then every such person and persons so doing and offending, their abettors, aiders, procurers, and counsellors, being thereof lawfully convicted and attainted according to the due order and course of the common laws of this

realm shall suffer specified penalties, culminating in punishment
for high treason on the third offence . .

There would be no going back even beyond the reign of Elizabeth.
For example, Sir Walter Raleigh was executed for aiding a Catholic
power as defined by this Act, although found guilty in another court
than that of the Church.[11] Here, the separation of Church and state in
Elizabeth's mind was unquestionable. Her Archbishop of Canterbury,
William Whitgift, was challenged by her bureaucracy led by her confidant, William Cecil. This gave Elizabeth no pleasure. If she were to be
supreme governor, head of the state Church here on earth and therefore
with divine power, the authority and controversies within and caused
by the Church were her responsibility, and none other should assume it
his.

There was, of course, unquestionable authority in Elizabeth's mind
that had been handed down from her father, Henry VIII. Yet there was
some sense that Elizabeth's Protestantism had none of the urgency
of Mary's Catholicism. Moreover, Elizabethan Protestantism had the
added irritation of the ethics of Puritanism, a movement that believed
the Catholic influence still had considerable standing in the state
Church and had to be purified. The Puritans were to demand absolute
change as soon as her death was announced and James VI of Scotland
began his journey to claim his throne as James I of England and the
title he preferred: the Union of the Crowns—Great Britain.

Almost the first claim on his duty as monarch, even before his coronation, was to judge the discontent written in the Millenary Petition, a
plea of demands signed supposedly by one thousand clergymen. He had
barely crossed from Berwick to England on his journey south to seek
his crown when the sheets and signatures were thrust upon him. The
Millenary Petition laid before him a charge among his clergy, exceed-
ingly militant on earth, that the Church of England was comfortable
and rehearsed many characteristics of the pre-Reformation; in this
his protesting priests were correct. The Church of England had not

[11] Raleigh (born c.1552) was convicted in 1603 (after Elizabeth's death that year) of
being in the pay of Catholic Spain, but was not executed until 1618.

abandoned the liturgical style of the Church of Rome. How could it have done? The liturgy was relatively simple and inoffensive. The wording of the Book of Common Prayer for the mass-cum-service of communion was easily followed by the Protestant persuasion—as still it is in the twenty-first century.

The Millenary priests accepted that prayer and acknowledgement of a greater God were understandable in any Christian rite; they could not accept the way in which the Church of Rome's liturgical theatre had not been written out of all forms of Protestant worship. As the form of worship was the way observed, agreed and authorised by the monarch, and no attempt had been made radically to alter that form, the petitioners were demanding that the monarch bring about the changes because only the monarch had the power to do so—the Church of England could not do it without instruction and authority of the king. The Puritans, in spite of their sense of liturgical austerity, knew that a king come to their bidding was unlikely, but that a king welcomed might hear their bidding prayers. Thus perhaps the Puritans chose the book of Esther for their passing flattery when they suggested the king's majesty might just have been ordained: 'We say with Mordecai to Hester, "Who knoweth whether you come to the kingdom for such a time?"'[12] Furthermore, the English priests were at odds with their supreme governor because he had been content to allow the Presbyterians to decide most aspects of Scottish everyday life. Given James's intellectual conceit, this Anglican view did not go unchallenged. In 1599 he had expressed forcibly his views in a paper, *Basilikon Doron*[13] *or His Majesties Instructions to his Dearest Sonne, Henry the Prince*, doubting the legitimacy of much of Puritan doctrine and especially the concept that quite small issues were, according to the Puritans, major concerns— for example, liturgical ritual, including the sign of the cross during baptism, bowing when the name Jesus was uttered and standards of preaching—and that had to be unequivocally corrected. In 1603, *Basilikon Doron* was published in England and it was James's belief that

---

[12] Esther iv.14.

[13] *Basilikon* from the Greek, meaning 'kingly', and *doran*, meaning 'gift'—in this case an instruction.

he had a divine right to reign and thus a God-ordained right to rule. A thousand clergy recognised James as the unquestioned head of the Church and implored him to be 'our physician to heal these diseases'. This was voiced and written acknowledgement that the Church's role and rule were subjects of the monarch's fancy. We are told a thousand signed the petition. The numbers matter not. The consequences were to live until the present as perhaps the single most important moment in English (and American?) literature, and would carry the authority and name not of the clergy but of the monarch as head of the Church. James was not much pleased at the lobbying of his Puritans; he did not like Puritans and believed them bent on destroying the Church as it was, in spite of their claims in the petition that their ambition was for change and not the bringing down of the king's most powerful institution:

> Your Majesty's most humble subjects, the ministers of the gospel, that desire, not a disorderly innovation, but a due and godly reformation...

James saw himself as an intellectual. Most certainly his tutors, the humourless, royalty-loathing, Kirk-worshipping child-beater, George Buchanan,[14] and the more liberal Peter (later Sir Peter) Young,[15] turned out a good scholar; if that were so, then he was the last of the line. No monarch since James's death in 1625 has displayed any surprising intellect. James's reasoning on the Church and its procedures was born in argument about the way of the Scottish persuasions. Yet he could not entirely ignore the case laid in the English petition.

His answer was very twenty-first century: he formed a committee of inquiry. In January 1604 James called together four thoughtful Puritans[16] and eighteen from the Church of England at Hampton Court. Thus the occasion is known as the Hampton Court Conference.

---

[14] 1506–82. He is remembered for *De jure regni apud Scotos* (1579), in which he opposed the notion of royal absolutism. James VI was not always in agreement with this concept.

[15] 1544–1628. He was also tutor to the future Charles I.

[16] Laurence Chaderton, Thomas Sparke, John Rainolds (Reynolds) and John Knewstubs.

The numbers of Puritans versus Church of England might be thought to have foretold a loaded conference. That would be a perfectly reasonable assumption were it not a reflection of the balance of Puritan and established churchmen of the day. Moreover, James had no real need to play politics with either group. He was confident that he would achieve what he wanted and certainly understood (as both sets of churchmen did) that changes would be good for the institution. Nevertheless, the loading did reflect James's mood and his reluctance to agitate the established Church, part of which recognised its shortcomings, but he was never going to judge them in conference with Puritans in case the Puritans gained an upper hand in reform. James's instincts were not far wrong. He felt this was not a Puritan ethic seeking liturgical management, but an outright attack on the established Church as an institution.

The Puritans were under no illusions about the king's mood. He had long made it clear that Puritanism was bad for the Church's soul and his political indigestion, conditions to which he had given considerable thought. As for the Catholics, if they had truly thought he would favour them (his mother being the Catholic Mary Queen of Scots) that was a dream too thin. James saw no reason to challenge Elizabeth's rule. The Puritans strictly believed that the Church liturgy could only hold those references that were in the scriptures. James, if not a disciple of his native Kirk then a student of its contradictions and uncompromising ways, was quite ready for the Puritan petition. He accepted that it apparently represented the views of ten per cent of his clergy and so had to be read, but he regarded it as mischievous. Yet James saw that some aspects could be agreed without overly upsetting the bishops, especially as reinforcing minor changes was difficult to monitor and verify.

The meeting that started on Monday 14 January 1604 was very much the sort of affair that is common among arbitrators in the present century. The two sides met separately. On day one the king met the bishops to see what they agreed to and on the second day it was the turn of the Puritans. The general demands were workable if not desirable. The Puritans wanted Church doctrine and administration to be scripture-based, better preachers and, most famously, a new translation of the Bible. Committees of scholars at Westminster, Cambridge and Oxford each worked on a section. The new translation was not an edited version of what was already in hand.

The scholars worked in the original languages, and the biblical and literary masterpiece was published in 1611. It appeared because only the monarch had the power to order it to be so and the power to approve or otherwise: a wise king once more, leading his Church. It could be that James I's decision to order the translation that became known as the Authorised Version was the final lasting influence over the liturgy and distinction of the state Church.

It was not the final act of a monarch's constitutional sense of integrity within that Church. The example of a crowning distinction of a monarch's duty as supreme governor came at the end of the eighteenth century. That sense of duty to the established Church meant a direct confrontation between king and Prime Minister; it was a conflict that only the supreme governor could win. Almost inevitably the cause of the schism was Ireland and Catholicism.

In the late eighteenth century, the move was on for Catholic emancipation in Ireland. In the 1790s, Ireland was a failing state that bred open rebellion by a mix of Presbyterians and Catholic defenders. The rebels fought for political independence and against the established Church.

Their demands included a law for Roman Catholic emancipation and another that would have encouraged the prominence of dissenters in radical politics. This was not a question of faith groups against a faithless ruling caste. For example, the Presbyterians opposed the episcopacy and a state Church of England and Ireland. In this opposition were the powerful arguments of the primacy of issues of Church polity over theology 'in shaping political outlooks'. The political aim was union between Ireland and Britain that no rebel cause wanted. The rebels, led by Protestants, wanted independence from British rule. The catalyst for union was the Irish rebellion of 1798, even though it was quickly put down. The inspiration of the rebels was the French Revolution, and their ambitions were independence from British rule and rejection of all state religion. Constitutional union of Great Britain and Ireland was seen by the then Prime Minister, William Pitt,[17] as a means of arresting the economic and political decline in Ireland, and countering the prospect of further open opposition against the state and the established Church, both in England and Ireland. Pitt believed union and emancipation went together. Such powerful and determined Presbyterian and Roman Catholic activists could not be ignored by a state with a Church established by parliamentary authority and with the monarch as its ruler on earth. Although not an issue of debate in England, it could not have gone unnoticed that to give Irish non-conformists more power through an Act of emancipation would have constitutional considerations that would also apply to English Catholics.

The English Catholics (lay-led as opposed to clergy-led, as in Ireland) were not agitators. Nevertheless, further Catholic emancipation inspired by events in rebellious Ireland could not be ignored in England. In Dublin, a further consideration had it that the Protestant ascendancy—the Dublin administration of British rule—should not have been seen as an anti-Irish estate marooned within the Dublin pale. The Protestant ascendancy was not a British expatriate society that automatically supported the will of crown and government. Many Protestants, including those in governing positions, were Anglo-Irish and valued their Irishness as much as their English heritage. They respected the limited independence the Dublin Parliament had enjoyed since the 1782 Catholic Relief Act, one of the Acts collectively known as the Constitution of 1782 that offered more legislative freedom to the Irish Parliament, but not absolute power. There had also been a suspicion in London of a Catholic conspiracy in Dublin Castle. The British had never allowed the Irish to have absolute parliamentary power.

The 1495 Poynings' Law (after the then viceroy, Edward Poynings) effectively meant that Westminster had to approve Bills, Acts and Requests. It was a procedure that had roused opposition in all centuries, including from the seventeenth-century Catholic Confederate Association, royalists loyal to the deposed Charles I, and from the Irish political leader, Henry Grattan (1746–1820), a loyalist and supporter

---

[17] 1759–1806.

of Catholic emancipation, and his late eighteenth-century Patriot Party. Laws against the rights to make laws for Ireland and legislation to prevent, for example, Catholics leaving their lands to a single heir were so effective that some Catholics even converted to Anglicanism in order to secure franchise and the future of their lands. The 1782 Catholic Relief Act had allowed Catholics to buy property and therefore have a holding big enough to qualify to vote.[18] Equally, the Act did not give Catholics the same rights as members of the established Church. A Catholic landowner could vote, but not sit in Parliament. The Catholics had won the right to vote for Anglican MPs and none other, because there was none other. Furthermore, any independence of the Dublin Parliament provided difficulties rather than political harmony between Britain and Ireland. For example, the Irish Parliament was able to obstruct proposals for the regency of George III.

The obstruction had consequences for the royal role as head of the established Church. Then there was a direct influence on many Irish of the French Revolution. Few would ignore that the French revolutionaries had abandoned the established Church of France, acknowledging that it was better existing alongside, rather than as part of, the new regime. In Ireland, the churches could be used to gather support for the dissenting movement that might otherwise have found it difficult to demand reforms of the Irish state's wider commercial, social and political condition. It was the religious grouping—in particular, the movement for Catholic emancipation—that became the unavoidable

---

[18] An act to 'enable his majesty's subjects of whatever persuasion, to testify their allegiance to him, ought to be considered as good and loyal subjects to his majesty, his crown and government; and whereas a continuance of several of the laws formerly enacted, and still in force in this kingdom, against persons professing the popish religion, is therefore unnecessary, in respect to those who have taken or shall take the said oath, and is injurious to the real welfare and prosperity of Ireland; therefore be it enacted ... that from and after the first day of May 1782 it shall and may be lawful to and for any person or persons professing the popish religion, to purchase, or take by grant, limitation, descent, or devise, and lands, tenements, or hereditaments in this kingdom, or any interest therein (except advowsons, and also except any manor or borough, or any part of a manor or borough, the freeholders or inhabitants whereof are entitled to vote for burgesses to represent such borough or manor in parliament) and the same to dispose of as he, she, or they shall think fit ...'

consideration in the debate. Prime Minister William Pitt the Younger had long argued for emancipation and in 1793 had secured concessions for Irish Roman Catholics but not emancipation. That Catholic emancipation did not coincide with the Act of Union did not lessen the religious influence on the decision to bring about union. These same religious influences and supporters were to be at the heart of the 1798 Rebellion.[19] For the English establishment and the Protestant ascendancy, religious identity could not be separated from politics and security of the state. The English had for at least three centuries identified Catholicism with their consistent enemies: Spain and France. Both states had sent soldiers into Ireland at different times in order to usurp England's authority and worse. George III's position was predictable and unequivocal: there would be no Catholic emancipation. William Pitt wrote to the king on 31 January 1801, making it clear that he regarded this as a resigning matter. So be it, said the king.

Queen's House [Greenwich], February 1, 1801
... a sense of religious as well as political duty has made me, from the moment I mounted the throne, consider the Oath that the wisdom of our forefathers has enjoined the Kings of this realm to take at their Coronation, and enforced by the obligation of instantly following it in the course of the ceremony with taking the Sacrament, as so binding a religious obligation on me to maintain the fundamental maxims on which our Constitution is placed, namely the Church of England being the established one, and that those who hold employment in the State must be members of it, and consequently obliged not only to take oaths

---

[19] In 1791, Wolfe Tone (1763–98), a Protestant Dublin lawyer together with other Protestant radicals in Belfast, including James Napper Tandy (1740–1803) and Thomas Russell (1767–1803), considerably inspired by the French Revolution and republican democracy in America, founded the Society of United Irishmen. Its original objective was parliamentary reform. However, while not an ecumenical group, the society, with its dissenter foundation, came together after Tone's pamphlet, *Argument on Behalf of the Catholics of Ireland*, arguing that religious division was exactly that, divisive, and so satisfied the ruling elite and that there should be Catholic, non-conformist and Protestant ecumenism.

against Popery, but to receive the Holy Communion agreeably to the rites of the Church of England.

This principle of duty must therefore prevent me from discussing any proposition tending to destroy this groundwork of our happy Constitution, and much more so that now mentioned by Mr Pitt [Catholic emancipation] which is no less than the complete overthrow of the whole fabric...

It was the last time that a monarch defended the Church of England over the wishes of his government, even to the point of losing his Prime Minister. To be the earthly head of the Church was not to be its pastor. Equally, the coronation oath was very clear and remained so, even if the wording toned down the grand description and claim on authority of the sovereign. Some kings after George III may not have behaved so clearly and may have given ground to Pitt the Younger. There is no reason to think that George IV would have had such a conscience on the matter.

In the twenty-first century, the monarch's position as governor of the state Church continued to be observed with dignity by state, Church and monarchy, and could do so because gradually all powers, other than ceremonial ones, were gradually removed from the monarch over two hundred years. If we return to the tablet of the monarchy that followed Elizabeth, we will see that the hand-in-hand monarchy and democratic process made waning powers inevitable, although Scotland's James VI, when he assumed the crown of England, would never have imagined that possible.

CHAPTER SEVEN

The Imported Monarchs

J ames VI of Scotland and I of England saw himself as monarch of
Great Britain. This was the Union of the Crowns, but not of the
countries. It was also a union of poor crowns. As previously mentioned,
the Scots had never had money. Elizabeth even had had to send plate for
the banquet to celebrate James's son's baptism. Rather like pre-1989,
penned-in eastern Europeans who heard travellers' tales and read
smuggled western magazines, and so thought everyone the other side of
the Berlin Wall was rich, sixteenth-century Scots believed everyone in
London and probably everyone in England was wealthy. Just as people
went from east to west to search for 1990 riches, so the Scots around
James VI went south to finger the gold lamé of privilege and join the
most cash-strapped industry in England: the Court.

James soon learned that one privilege of monarchy was the need to
find the money to feed his Court. Everyday kitchen table victuals meant
maintaining forty tables of food and beers and wines. The likes of the
Erskines, who had travelled south with James, expected to join the
lords' and ladies' tables every day, often with forty dishes at each table.
The senior courtiers, the Lord Chamberlain and the Lord Treasurer
et al, would have their own tables and people to feed. All would come
out of the king's coffers. This is worth recording because four hundred
years later the monarch has still to provide for the staff of palaces and

houses. Perhaps the daily eating and drinking are on a more modest scale, but they are, just as the almost unsuspecting James VI discovered, an expensive part of sovereign accounting.

James is mostly remembered for the Authorised Version of the Bible and escaping the apparent ambitions of Guido Fawkes. He should be more commonly remembered for bringing the two crowns together. When he went to Parliament in March 1604, James made an indisputable point: in becoming monarch he had united people with one language, one Church and similar ways, hitherto separated by a border that few followed with any assurances, although the dialect was quite distinct, as it is four centuries later, with people a few yards either side of the border speaking very differently. The new king saw his right to rule as God-given. Therefore he supposed that to ignore his thoughts that union of two crowns should go the extra stage—England and Scotland as one people—was to ignore divine wishes. Parliament was politely and firmly unimpressed. There were two important considerations that James had hardly considered. Few in the corridors of Court and Parliament were entirely happy with a Scottish monarch. They were reluctant to welcome the Scots at Court and saw them, and their womenfolk, as barely socially acceptable, rude, demanding and money-grabbing. In short, few magnates wished to be ruled by a Scot, even if the line of royal succession was indisputable; English anti-Scottishness in 1604 was as obvious as it is in the second decade of the twenty-first century.

Moreover, there was a distinct understanding (or at least a belief) that James's reasoning meant that England and Scotland would disappear, to be replaced by one country called Britain or Great Britain. Presumably, therefore, all laws—political, constitutional and case—would be history and because of the authority of the monarch in the opening years of the seventeenth century, James would have the last word on the new laws to govern this new realm. Hardly surprisingly, Parliament firmly but politely turned down the king's demands for union. It would not come for another century, in 1707.

James was defeated in his great cause, but with his power of royal prerogative he styled himself King of Great Britain and called the heralds to design a new royal standard giving the unicorn of Scotland equal prominence with the lion of England. On the new flag, because it was done in this king's name, James was heraldically 'Iacomus', hence 'Jacobus', which is where the term 'Union Jack' comes from. James I was clever: making union by stealth maybe. It would have stood a better chance if he had had any money. Elizabeth left England with no reserves. So he went back to Parliament where all monarchs had to go for money; indeed, most monarchs saw raising money as the only sound reason for Parliament. Parliament said no. If James thought he could get taxes without Parliament's consent he had failed to understand that its members were always going to oppose him; to do otherwise would have established a precedent that would have meant their irrelevance. On these occasions, James invoked the name of God. He ruled by divine right. He was head of the state Church, so who better to say this? He failed and thus all but accepted the way things were, including the fact that the Scottish relations and hangers-on in the bedchamber were all but bankrupting him. That was the way of rule until James's death in 1625 and the coming of his son, Charles, to the throne.

Charles liked the elaborate trappings and finery of monarchy. He would not have subscribed to the idea of being a people's monarch. Apart from his own delights he understood full well, unlike some modern royalty, that the people do not want a people's version of anything. They have the people's version themselves. Part of the attraction of monarchy to many, though not all, is that it provides the pageantry beyond all but the most privileged. As Charles remarked in the most difficult circumstances (seconds before his execution), a subject and a sovereign are clearly different things. Moreover, when the crown is six hundred years old, it is to be admired. It is not a Bond Street or a Fifth Avenue bauble. Charles I at just twenty-six began his reign with the most elaborate coronation at Westminster Abbey, on 2 February 1626, with 'all the splendour, solemnity and sacred mysteries of the medieval Catholic rite'.[1] It would end in equally spectacular fashion with his brilliant, white-laced head on the black-masked executioner's block outside the Banqueting House in Whitehall on 30 January 1649, after Parliament

---

[1] Starkey, David, *Monarchy: From the Middle Ages to Modernity*, p.102, Harper Press, London, 2006.

had, with haste, passed a Bill making it a treasonable offence to declare, or declare for, a successor.

Charles I was a failed political monarch. He could never have given quiet counsel on the events of the day, although he most certainly could have gone on for some time about the beauty in a drawing, a colour, a silk, a delicately stitched tapestry. Charles I, hardly an imposing figure and one of considerable shyness, was an aesthete. He was the perfect example of one of the challenges for the people at the time of a monarch's passing, whether it was in tenth-century Saxon times or the twenty-first century: the new monarch never mirrors the triumphs, failures or even the styles of the previous monarch. To ask if the next-in-line will be any good as king, or queen, is a fruitless pondering. The unique position of a monarch in society means comparisons are odious and, as the British Houses of Hanover, Saxe-Coburg-Gotha and Windsor have proven, the monarch in waiting often waits uneasily and even mischievously. Charles I was not his father and certainly not an acolyte. Like his father, he was short of money and never going to get it from Parliament, especially as he wanted to go to war, and he increased his unpopularity by marrying Princess Henrietta Maria, both a Catholic and a Frenchwoman. In more recent descriptive, that might have been seen as toxic politics. The English Parliament, as with most of these new assemblies where they existed throughout Europe, sat when the monarch called them to do so. Literally, the sovereign's writ ran.

Charles saw little need for Parliament. His view that such a legislature was obstructive and certainly not always willing to pass tax-raising legislation was one shared with many others in continental Europe. However, unlike political chambers in Europe, the British Parliament could not to be ignored. The monarch needed Parliament and Parliament was the keystone to political advancement in these islands that was seemingly ahead of anything anticipated across the Channel. The king did not have the ability to raise taxes. In theory, only Parliament could and only that place had the authority and means of backing up the tax-raising legislation. Charles saw matters entirely differently. He extended the single tax that was easy to collect and had some tradition behind it. England as an island state was vulnerable to seaborne attack and the major ports paid a tax to raise the not inconsiderable sums needed to build the fleets that had protected the English coastline, not always successfully, since Saxon times. This funding was part of the money used to raise fleet money, or Ship Money, in Elizabeth's time, and in theory, at least, had been justified with the defeat of the Armada in 1588. The money came from ports. Charles, or certainly his attorney William Noy, argued that the hinterland towns should also pay their way towards England's fleet defences.

By 1635, the tax was so successful that it was producing almost all of the money Charles had wanted Parliament to sanction. When some objected to the monarch's right to raise money without parliamentary consent, the king's response was that he had the right because, as king, he had a duty to defend and preserve the realm. How that should be done and would be paid for was the king's duty to decide. This was a ruler overturning the authority of a legislative assembly with origins in the Model Parliament of 1295, although with hardly any of the authority understood in the twentieth century. Charles I's Parliament was still only called at the king's pleasure.

The anxieties of Parliament expressed over Charles's supposed divine right to rule were threefold. Charles was unquestionably a patron of all things artistic in the broadest sign and his feelings for all that was beautiful suggest a personality of some other time or, most likely, some other place. He would have enjoyed Medici Florence. Unlike the Medici, Charles was not a wise king. He relied on Noy, and successfully. He achieved what he wanted, but misunderstood the value that Parliament could be for the crown in more difficult times. Parliament was not a place of republicanism, but it would not stand aside when Charles embarked on his most perilous constitutional expedition. For Parliament, regal peradventure could only lead to disaster, although few would have imagined the tragedy of it all when Charles, or maybe more particularly his Archbishop of Canterbury, William Laud, set out to restore the whole communion of Churches to what both saw as splendid liturgy as opposed to the raw-boned way of something close to Puritanism and, more disconcertingly to the Laudian view, leanings towards the ways of the Scottish Kirk. In short, Laud and Charles (with his Catholic wife) were for leading the Church of England back to the ways of Roman Catholicism, or so many thought; that it could be little more than regal delight and vanities of liturgical pageantry mattered not.

The effects of Charles's belief in God-blessed reform and Laud's support did not bring about rebellion. In the deaneries, change was superficial and dissent not particularly widespread. Probably because Laud (and Charles) 'got away with it' in England, they pressed their royal and clerical case in Scotland. The risks were unquestionable. Scottish forms of worship could not be compared to those south of the border. A divinely appointed Charles I saw himself as head of everything. In 1633 he appointed Scottish episcopal bishops and in 1635 Edinburgh was declared a diocese, with William Forbes its first bishop. However, Scotland was not afraid of royal patronage. Scotland was raw Reformation and Charles was not supreme anything in the Kirk, and the revised and more gaudily expressed English prayerbook would most certainly cause uproar when in 1637 it was presented for use in the mother church of Presbyterianism, Saint Giles, High Kirk of Edinburgh. There was a riot and a real one. The sentiment spread every time the prayerbook was read in services almost anywhere in Scotland. It would not be accurate to make a comparison with modern times and gatherings in squares that lead to something more volatile: yet without, then, the uses of social media, that is more or less what happened next.

The protesters would not go away. What had been a simple if noisy and heartfelt occasion became heavily politicised. The political and religious movers and shakers set a covenant to oppose and set aside what they saw as an evil act. That covenant became the birthmark of the protest. Here was the origin of the Covenanters, whose factions ruled Scotland for thirteen years between 1638 and 1651. From these factions came the Kirk Party, extremists who grabbed much power but because of splits within splits of the radical elements, they could never hold together for long enough to consolidate into a long ruling party. In the earlier days of the Covenanters, their groups from the Lowlands did spread enough powerful influence and radical opinion until they controlled the Church and that meant they would effectively control Scotland albeit not for long. The made demands on the English monarch that Charles dismissed and said he would rather die than give in. If Charles had given in he may have died in old age; what had started as a folly-expressed-too-far in Scotland became a cause in England that would bring him and Laud to the scaffold.

The mood among the magnates in England (Parliament had not been called by Charles for a decade) reflected a belief by the English *nomen-klatura* that this was no eccentricity of a king best left to his assumption of God's appointment and his van Dycks, but the blatant attempt to reintroduce Catholicism. It was the monarch's all but empty treasury that signalled the events that would bring about revolution. Ship Money could not produce the funds the king needed and he was forced to call Parliament in 1640. That meant that the collective argument against voting for more taxes to set the army on the Scots would inevitably spill into the debate of creeping Catholicism. This is exactly what happened. The Puritans set the stage with support settling about the member for Tavistock, John Pym, and his documented claims that the king's doing during the previous ten years or so had been against the religious and constitutional condition of nonconformist England. Charles did what he might be expected to do with such opposition: after a month of its recall, he dissolved Parliament—hence its historical label as the Short Parliament. If that did not create anger and then turmoil, the invasion of England by the Scottish army and its entry as far south as Newcastle took care of those who might have doubted Charles's motives and capability to serve as a good king with a duty of quietly governing his people.

Charles was forced to reconvene Parliament. Its members demanded that he give up all but the loose change from his Ship Money tax; Laud was dismissed from the Court and Parliament demanded that Catholics should be sent from the bedchamber counsel of Queen Henrietta Maria, and importantly that the episcopate should be abandoned and bishops dismissed.

At this moment, we might look at the historical reference that makes some sense today. The undoing of the basic structure and authority of the state Church was a reform too far for Charles, as it had been for his father James. As we shall see, the disestablishment of the Church of England movement, supported as it is among some senior clergy, questions one of the last traditional roles of the monarch, the Church's governor. Charles then (but with less authority), as his father had before him, declaimed that without bishops there could be no king. Disestablishment of the state Church in the twenty-first century would not include doing away with mitres, but it certainly would be doing away with one of the functions of the monarch.

James had talked about the Puritan demands of him that the clergy be restructured to exclude bishops. He said: 'I know what would become of my supremacy...No bishop, no king. When I mean to live under presbytery I will go to Scotland again.'[2]

In the circumstances of 1640 Charles I could not retreat to Scotland, but he could, with few political options left, deal with the Scots. The following year, he went to Edinburgh and agreed that he would remove bishops. As we know, his surrender to Scottish *Realpolitik* was not the reassurance of a peaceful and uninterrupted reign he may have expected. The surrender in Edinburgh had the opposite result in England, where the Pymites were now in confrontation with Charles's supporters. John Pym laid before Parliament what in later times might be called a no-confidence vote. Pym took what he thought to be the wrongs of Charles's reign and laid them out in the Grand Remonstrance of 1641. This was more than a vote of confidence, or lack of it. This was in effect the manifesto of Charles's opponents and one of the earliest forms of opposition in parliamentary history. It went through by eleven votes and was printed. Charles was likely to accept neither the document nor its sentiment, and the division between Puritan Parliamentarians and Royalists was cemented.

It is not our purpose to go into the story and the Civil War. The time spent on Charles I shows the point at which Saxon kingship was finally discarded or, at least, waned and that the English came to a conclusion that, however monarchy might exhibit the most destabilising frailties, the nation state needed at very least its symbolism as the unifying force. A modern argument for preserving the monarchy is based on the neutrality of the king or queen and the monarch as an unambitious constant in public life. The rebellion that started in August 1642 against monarchy failed because the alternative could not provide that constant. The standards were raised; families and regions split loyalties; regicide stained the cause; and by 1660 it was clear that the king's health was, once again, a toast without fear of retribution.

The eleven-year experiment in an English republic had run its course. The clear line between leadership and dictatorship was a fudge. A form of democracy was slowly to emerge, whereby at least two opposite views

---

[2] Willson, David Harris, *King James VI & I*, p.198, Jonathan Cape, London, 1956.

could be debated rather than struck bloodily and the people openly side with one or the other without physical threat. However, in the 1660s none would even imagine a road to universal suffrage; but the April 1660 Declaration of Breda was a further and reasonably assured step on the control of the power of the monarchy.

By signing the declaration, Charles II absolved those who had opposed the crown. Apart from financial arrangements he promised there would not be suppression of religious minorities. That could include Catholics, but it was more importantly a recognition of those persuasions outside the Church of England. The terms of the agreement were to be ratified by Parliament. Without the parliamentarian and parliamentary vote, the return of the monarch (the monarchy had always been there but in exile) could not have been achieved with another political upheaval. There remained a single most important element of the return to England under a monarch: the Restoration was a Protestant Restoration. When the first Parliament of the Restoration was formed it indicated that the nonconformist agitators of the rebellion and the Commonwealth were, in retrospect, the losers in the peaceful moments of the new constitutional monarchy. Parliament was now under the control of Royalists.

Charles II's reign, his childless marriage to the Portuguese Catherine of Braganza, his considerable number of illegitimate children, the regal poverty that had him selling Dunkirk to the French (1662), with Sweden and the Dutch Republic his part in the Triple Alliance against France, and his duplicity by entering a secret pact with Louis XIV are reminders that his was hardly a quarter-century rule of a king content with foppery and pleasures. For our purpose, it was the uncertainty of the Protestant value of England that marks the importance of Charles II, who fought a Parliament opposed to allowing the crown to pass to his brother, James, Duke of York, who had married the Catholic Mary of Modena. Charles sent Parliament away and ruled without that assembly until his death as a Catholic in 1685.

Charles was succeeded by his brother, James II. At first sight, all was well. Parliament voted him virtually everything he asked for, including money, and his support appeared unwavering. Considering that everyone surely knew what they were getting—the first openly Catholic monarch since Mary Tudor—it says much for the respect of the position of monarch that the opposition was not immediately in revolt. What went wrong?

James was the surviving son of Charles I and Henrietta Maria. He had gone into exile during the Civil War and returned at the Restoration to be Lord High Admiral and to marry Anne Hyde, and so be father to two future queens, Mary II and Anne. There were of course some adjustments to be made once the Restoration was established. James was a Catholic and the state, through the Test Act passed during Charles II's reign and seen by the bishops as the very guarantor of the state Church, forbade Catholics holding high office. In 1673 James resigned all offices rather than renounce his Catholicism. However, once king, he defied his parliamentarians and began finding offices for Catholics. If any further alarm bells might be rung, in 1688 James Francis Stuart was born and became Catholic heir to the throne. Imagine the years of religious paranoia in England and the determination, among those who could, to stop a Roman Catholic even sitting on the British throne. Yet for James II, it all began well enough.

His coronation on Saint George's Day was full of bells, smoke, laces and the music of Henry Purcell. Not everyone of influence was at the service. Most importantly, the Duke of Monmouth, one of Charles II's bastards, was in exile in the Republic of the Seven United Netherlands—the Dutch Republic—with the anti-Catholic faction of Whigs.[3] Monmouth, by most accounts a reluctant revolutionary, sailed that spring from the Netherlands for Dorset where he had expected to raise forces to march on James II's army. It was an inept expedition, and after his barely trained and continuously inept troops were routed at the Battle of Sedgemoor in Somerset in July 1685. Monmouth was found hiding in a ditch. Unfortunately for Monmouth, shortly after landing he had declared himself King James II. His treason was therefore self-convicting; in spite of begging for the rightful monarch's mercy, he went to the Tower, and after five blunt and inexpert axe-blows his head was cut with a knife from his wretched torso. James felt reassured and

---

[3] The terms 'Whig' and 'Tory' have been used since the seventeenth century, and were pejorative terms that their holders came to like. Tories came from a disreputable band of Irish bandits and Whigs were 'whiggamors', Scottish cattle drivers.

victorious, and full of divine energy and Blessing for his rule. He was wrong.

James had done well with his army against Monmouth and had done so with the help of Catholic officers. At the time, that was not an unreasonable reinforcement during a state of national emergency. But the Test Act had not been abandoned. Parliament could be sent away, but the courts could not. That was no matter if the judiciary were packed with James's yes-men. The sympathetic judiciary now pronounced that monarchs could set aside laws if the throne thought it best to do so. England was back in a dictatorship, which had the judges ruling that refusal to do the king's bidding—even in a matter that appeared to go against the law of the land—was effectively, treason. Moreover, James was no desperate king. His coffers were well stocked. His army was drilled enough. His belief that God marched with him in the name of Catholicism was unwavering. His belief and determination faced stiff opposition from the Anglican bishops, Parliament and the law. The constitutional and religious conundrum was further complicated by news that Mary of Modena, James's second wife, had given birth to a son on 10 June 1688. This was baby James Francis, the English throne's Catholic heir. Or was he? Many, including James's Protestant daughter Anne, disbelieved the baby was born of this Mary.

In the Netherlands, the heir presented a difficulty for *stadhouder* Willem Hendrik van Oranje-Nassau, otherwise William of Orange, James's son-in-law by his marriage to the king's daughter, Mary. William of Orange wanted the English throne because he wanted English money and English armies to defend his lands against the Catholic advances of the French. Could a legitimate heir claim the throne instead of Mary? Perhaps with these doubts, William was forced into the decision to invade England to chase his father-in-law away and claim the throne.

William landed in England on 5 November in Devon. Two of James's best commanders, John Churchill (ancestor of Winston and future Duke of Marlborough), and Anne's husband, Prince George of Denmark, went over to the invading William of Orange. It was a very curious affair. The king was still king, but he had gone. His daughter had come, but she was not queen. William was a distant heir, fourth in line, and the Tories in particular used this as a good reason to ignore any claim making the throne Mary's and not William's. Also, what about the royal baby? That was the simplest difficulty to resolve. Parliament, without implicitly and certainly not explicitly getting involved in the gossip of the bairn's parentage and claims, expressed the view that a Catholic monarch was not the English way. That was not entirely so. Parliament was saying that the nation's experience suggested that the Book of Common Prayer's hope for the people to be quietly governed would be better met if the monarch were other than a Catholic. The vacancy for monarch was there for all to see, but the incumbent was still enthroned, if absent. It was not a situation that could last and did not. Parliament could not be called, because only the king could do that, but its members gathered to institute a compromise that would have surprised neither Saxons nor Danes. William, not for one moment willing to be consort, could rule as proper sovereign, but jointly with Mary. With Mary's crown, the Stuart succession was in theory honoured. 'In theory' was good enough for that moment.

William was preoccupied with the defence of the Netherlands against the French. To accept the opportunities in England—whose troops he wanted for his war against Louis XIV's France—would tactically leave his homeland vulnerable. In the circumstances it looked as if he should remain in continental Europe. What should an ambitious prince do? The matter was resolved when Louis invaded Germany. Relieved of fears of French action, William made sail for England. Just as William of Normandy had been pinned to his own coastline for days in October 1066 before the wind shifted and he could sail his invasion fleet for the Sussex coast, William in October 1688 was wind-bound on the Dutch coast until a force four veered, and he too could bring his fleet across and down the Channel to land out of James's way on the beaches of Torbay.

The importance of that moment in British seventeenth-century constitutional history was evident once the principle of William and Mary's reign had been decided. For the second time in just forty years, Parliament had removed a legitimate British monarch; the difference this time was clear: Parliament had decided he was not the right one for Britain and the British, and had given the throne to someone of whom they approved. Moreover, the principal cause for constitutional change was religion, more specifically the fear of Catholic rule that would usurp the authority of the state Protestant Church, but could link Britain too closely with the ambitions of Catholic France and even Spain. The arrival of William was in effect a *de facto* invasion. Moreover, Parliament had made way for that invasion, not this time from Normandy whence William I had arrived with the claim that Edward the Confessor had promised him the throne of England, but from the Netherlands. This was a further statement of the Henrican Tudor insistence that Britain's Protestant Church existed by order of Parliament, not by the evangelism of its clergy. That Parliament also ordained that the state Church should be defended as an unambiguous persuasion, and would have as its earthly governor and defender an equally unambiguously Protestant monarch. Clearly, there was more to this than a constitutional housekeeping moment in the way in which the British officially worshipped and saluted.

Parliament was stating what would have been a basic tenet in a written British constitution—had there been one: Parliament was telling the known world that Britain was Protestant from throne to kitchen drudge, and that other Christian persuasions could be tolerated, but strictly as minorities, most certainly not as equals. Importantly in retrospect, this was the moment that, having lived for centuries with the fear of invasion, the British were inviting foreign princes to be monarchs of all they could survey in the British Isles, even if—as in the case of the first Hanoverian, George I—the sovereign from over the water spoke little or no English. This was the state of England during the closing of the seventeenth century, when the enormous and sometimes dangerous powers of the monarchy were waning, and giving way to the commercial, mercantile and embryonic colonial interests of what would become by the second half of the new century a recognisable form of parliamentary government. In just forty years the then pejorative term 'Prime Minister' was used to describe the First Lord of the Treasury (Robert Walpole), although it would be towards the end of that century before the Prime Minister (Pitt the Younger) would be indisputably the head of Cabinet government.

In 1688 we can see that the moment of William and Mary's accession was not the beginning of Westminster democracy, but that it was a proper historical milestone in the changing relationship between monarch and state that would bring it about. There was a single factor in that relationship that had completely changed from the times of all

The Protestant William III, Prince of Orange and his wife Queen
Mary enthroned in 1689 at the overthrow of the Catholic James
II, at the behest of Parliament.

earlier monarchs. The typical political lie of the land no longer presented a predictable attitude to monarchy. Before William and Mary, very much a generalisation would be: Tories unquestionably supported the monarchy with its absolute claims of divine right to rule while Whigs were against that absolute power claimed by successive sovereigns. The arrival of William, probably more than his Stuart wife Mary, challenged these distinctions.

Tories were confused. They rightly supposed they supported the monarch. But had they not been devoted to the person they saw as constitutional successor to Charles II, James? The Tory instinct was to be wary of anything that smacked of revolution and 1649, a period many of them had witnessed. The Whigs had problems enough with James II, or any monarch for that matter. To have an invader on the throne via his Stuart wife was too confusing to a group that was not politically dysfunctional, any more than the Tories were. The common parliamentary unease about the circumstances of the William and Mary accession produced considerable ambition to enforce terms and conditions on the new rulers, and not fall into the Restoration trap of being so pleased to have got themselves a monarch again that they all but emptied the coffers into the king's Treasury.

The single moment to judge the step-change in the role of monarchy and the emerging powers of Parliament could well be the revision of the Triennial Act. There were in fact three Triennial Acts. The first was agreed while Charles I still had his head. As we have noted earlier, only the king could summon Parliament. Parliament did not have the routine of meeting all the time other than during elections, as now it does. In 1641, Parliament and the king agreed that Parliament could not be dismissed by the monarch and sent into recession until it suited the sovereign to recall the assembly—often when the king needed money that Parliament only could sanction. The first Triennial Act stated that Parliament was to sit for at least fifty days and, more importantly, it could not be dissolved for more than three years at a time.

Three years later, an amendment to the Act stated that Parliament must meet at least once every three years. It was a fruitless amendment and with the new monarchs a new agreement was struck. The 1694 Triennial Act had Parliament meeting at least once every three years and sitting for not more than three years. It is not truly certain how

William felt about the 1694 Act, but it would be likely that as long as Parliament gave him the money to prosecute his war against the French in the Netherlands, he would see his lot as a good bargain. He was not as fussed as Mary's family about the trappings and regalia of monarchy, but this was now four years on since Parliament had restricted the money he could expect from the most powerful taxer in British history, Customs and Excise.

Parliament had few options. William had arrived in England as a Dutch prince at war with France. By making him English monarch, Parliament found itself and the English buying into William's war. Britain, at William's declaration, was now at war with France. The expense of war was crippling. The stone monuments of the war are still to be seen and reflect the enormity of it. The Old Admiralty Building in Whitehall, Queen Mary's Royal Hospital for wounded and retired sailors on the Thames at Greenwich (now the University of Greenwich), and Mercer's Hall for the newly founded Bank of England give some lasting notion of the financial, constitutional and social revolution that came with the reign of William and Mary.

That William was an important English monarch should not be disputed. He was, though, a largely unpopular one, openly mocked as Hook Nose. Why would he have been liked? He was foreign; his ambitions for English troops and money to fight his own battles were not at all hidden and so despised; he was an expensive sovereign and, almost unforgivably to the English, he cared hardly a fig for royal pageant and spectaculars, thanks to his own personality. His wife, a true Stuart, was the people's monarch and much mourned when she died of smallpox in 1694. If the French thought his undoubted unpopularity in England would be to their advantage, they were misguided. William was never going to be removed by Parliament and for eight years the war in Europe dragged on, with a convenient truce in 1697, as did William's uneasy relationship with his adopted people. In 1702 he fell off his horse, died and was buried, in virtual secrecy, late at night, in Westminster Abbey. William was an underrated influence on the relationship between Church, state and monarchy. His reign was a time of constitutional restructuring and directly from it came the debate on the priorities of all three great institutions that has survived into present times.

CHAPTER EIGHT

The Coming of the Hanoverians

Q ueen Mary's sister, Anne, became queen and England took to her mostly because she was not William and famously made it very clear that she was above all 'entirely English'. Considering that Anne was the last of the Stuart line on the English throne, her Scottishness had not been lost over a century. In practical regal terms Anne was unremittingly Protestant, popularly a champion of the war against France, and blessed with wisdom and urging from her then close friend, Sarah Churchill, when it came to appointing a general to carry on the campaign. Reluctantly, William had, shortly before his unseating in the park beyond Hampton Court, reinstated Sarah's husband, John Churchill, as his commander. Anne confirmed his appointment.

The story of Churchill's victories at, most famously Blenheim and Ramillies and Oudenarde, are for elsewhere. Significantly for the progression of the monarchy, Anne's son, William, died in 1700. The succession of Protestant English-Scottish monarchy unnerved the British (from the 1707 Union with Scotland), particularly as the usurped monarch, James II, had died in exile in France in 1701 in France, still an enemy. Furthermore, William III was still king and therefore the mystery of James's son's birth remained an issue; James Francis was born in 1688 or was smuggled in a warming pan into the queen's chamber, as some would have it. The French recognised him as

James III of England and James VIII of Scotland. The English recognised James Francis as a Catholic pretender; indeed, later he was referred to as the Old Pretender. His supporters, getting their title from the Latin of his name, were the Jacobites, and Parliament, with its history of playing with the fire of musical thrones, made certain that the description of the successor would be written into English constitutional law when in 1701 the Act of Settlement was passed. It had one simple, understood principle: no English monarch should be a Roman Catholic. More particularly, future monarchs had to be Protestants, and admirers and members of the state Church of England. But given the limitations of searching for a monarch from the Tudor-Stuart line, where would Parliament find such an heir to the throne? 'No Catholics need apply' was the written condition, but of course they did.

The choices were few for the English Parliament and they settled on yet another non-English candidate, James I's granddaughter, Sophia of Hanover. Here was the origin of the Hanoverians in England, although Sophia would not live to sit on the English throne or even set foot in England, in case the people took to her and factions for her developed. There would be no English spring in Anne's realm. Scotland, however, might be a matter beyond her control, especially as the Act of Settlement had been an entirely English affair that was imposed on the Scots who, after all, only had a Parliament in name but no influence. What if the Scots, not yet in union with England (there was only a union of crowns), decided on total independence?

In 1703, the issues were not the same as 2014, but the debate was as strong. The Scots claimed that the next monarch of England need not be the sovereign of Scotland. The Parliament in London had the measure of the Scots and passed the 1706 Aliens Act whereby any Scots living in England were fine, but those living at home in Scotland should be described as aliens. It was a threat whose bones were constitutionally brittle. Its purpose was to scare the Scots and bring everyone together in an Act of Union with both nations to be in Great Britain, the term first used more than a century earlier by James VI of Scotland as he travelled from Berwick to claim the English throne. In 2013, the government in London started a monthly scare-the-Scottish-voters campaign to convince Scots there were no advantages in independence. On May Day 1707 the Act of Union became the law of the two lands.

The bringing together of Scotland and England in 1707 was the constitutional and political achievement of Anne's reign. In the summer of 1714 she died, aged forty-nine. In 1715, the Old Pretender made a hopeless attempt to claim the throne. He proclaimed himself James VIII and III, but had weak support, and in February the following year the would-be monarch deserted his followers and sailed for France. Instead of a pretender, the real monarch, albeit one who could speak no English and apparently never wished to, arrived from Hanover to be crowned and decorated as George I.

The Guelf family were rulers of the Brunswick duchies. This was the House of Hanover that reigned over Britain from 1714 until the last Hanoverian, Victoria, died in 1901. There were four Georges. The first did not like the English and at any opportunity retreated to his home-lands, but pocketed many English funds for his mistresses. The second George needed the British army to fight for him on the continent and is regularly cited as the last British monarch to lead his troops into battle (or certainly to be with them). This was at Dettingen in 1743 during the War of Austrian Succession (1740–48). He never much got on with his father, George I, and set up an opposing Court in his own home, Leicester House.

His reign was another step-change in British constitutional history inasmuch as George II did listen to his ministers and act upon their advice, and he eventually left the politics of Britain very much to the emerging political élite as no other monarch had done before him. He was followed by his grandson, who became George III. This king's image and reputation have been unfairly treated in modern times because of the not entirely historically accurate English drama, *The Madness of King George*, and the assumption therein that the king was deranged; it was his unsound medical treatment that created that myth, reinforced by the need for a regency, the process of having the next-in-line rule in his absence. He is also remembered as the monarch who 'lost' England's first colony, America. Religious reformers also criticise George III for preventing Pitt the Younger bringing in a Bill for Catholic emancipation. But he did so because he defended his coronation oath in which he promised to defend the Church of England.

Critical works about George III should be treated with caution. George III's England shuddered for a decade and more after the

The burning of the Bastille, 14 July 1789, was to be part
of the inspiration for the Irish Rebellion in 1798.

execution of Louis XVI of France in 1793, even though the British
at first saw this as a welcome sign that France was 'modernising'.
Although some continued with that view, the majority gradually
settled into that terrible political and constitutional uncertainty,
the fear of outside influence. Just as the Arab Spring demonstrations
of 2011 onwards spread alarm that nowhere in the region was safe
from protest, so in late eighteenth- and early nineteenth-century
England and Britain a question with similar fear of the answer was
asked: could the revolution spread to England? There were certainly
many who thought so and many who wanted it to do so. The 1798
Irish rebellion, a mainly Protestant affair, was partly inspired by what
had gone on in France and the new ideas of republican democracy as
practised in the by then United States of America. Differences among
the British political intelligentsia included the long-held criticism of
George III by Edmund Burke when he wrote in 1770 that the king was

disrupting democracy by ruling without considering the developing party-political system;[1] then, separately, there was his contradictory text condemning the events in France twenty years on, *Reflections on the French Revolution*. His views were opposed by his one-time friend, Charles James Fox,[2] who openly supported the reasoning behind the French Revolution. Little wonder that the events in Paris were even a tourist attraction for London.

George III's eldest son, and regent when his father was unable to rule in 1811, became George IV on the death, after a decade incapacitated, of his father in June 1820. Thus ended a reign of sixty years during which the constitutional monarchy, the base of the Industrial Revolution, commercial and colonial expansion, and the invention of modern politics came at a pace never imagined in the time of the first Hanoverian, and probably not so rapidly until the post-First World War period.

George IV should be remembered as a prince of enormous potential who ran to obesity and opium; he is best remembered—and is thus perhaps forgotten—for his wastefulness, a sordid adultery trial (to rid himself of his queen, Caroline), hypocrisy, public contempt, indolence and scandal. He died to a silence of tears in June 1830 to be succeeded by George III's third son, the Duke of Clarence, a sixty-four-year-old sailor prince with a mistress, Dorothea Jordan; together, they had ten children. He became William IV in 1830. This was the period of great political and constitutional change. Certainly, it was a monarchy with a social and ceremonial difference. If twenty-first-century monarchy dumbing-downers want an English precedent, William IV comes close. Like most sailors, William kept most ceremonials to a minimum. He was impatient with palace trappings and indifferent to a coronation. He would have been quite happy with a signing ceremony and as he was the only one allowed to wear the crown, was that not recognition enough? The horror of all this among palace and Court jobsworths may be imagined, just as it might in the twenty-first century. No wonder the late Lord Nelson had got on with him. William IV's peace and quiet was not to be disturbed by bows and scrapes and the occasions of Court dress

---

[1] *Thoughts on the Cause of the Present Discontents.*
[2] 1749–1806.

and undress. His opening months as king coincided with an onslaught of constitutional revolution in Parliament.

Inside seven years of William's reign there was barely a month when a political debate or scientific and social achievement did not rewrite the way in which the British identity was seen abroad. The great Duke of Wellington became Prime Minister and then fell to be succeeded in the Whig revolution by Earl Grey. The determination of a majority to reform the parliamentary system and that of others to oppose it ebbed and flowed as the Lords rejected reform, people took to the streets against the Lords' decision and the king was forced into the contrived solution of threatening to create new peers to vote for reform. The Bill became an Act in 1832. The 1829 Catholic Emancipation Act became law in the year William became king and a supposed Abolition of Slavery Bill was passed into law in 1833.

As well as this political march towards a fairer society, others were changing the way that society looked and felt about the future. Charles Lyell published his *Principles of Geology*, William Cobbett his *Rural Rides* and Charles Dickens his *Sketches by Boz*. Michael Faraday began his work on electricity and Charles Darwin began his voyages in *The Beagle*. And if all this were too electrifying, in 1834 the Houses of Parliament burned down and William IV became the last monarch in England to 'sack' his Prime Minister when he dismissed Lord Melbourne and told Robert Peel to form an administration. In that seven-year reign, the relationship and style of monarch, the people and Parliament changed. When the eighteen-year-old Princess Victoria ascended the throne in 1837, there was little wonder that she needed such wise counsel from her reluctant but adoring Prime Minister, Lord Melbourne. Melbourne was a Whig. Victoria was a Whig by influence and by instinct. It was a good pairing and did well for three years, even though Victoria made certain that Melbourne stayed by her side when Peel should have been Prime Minister. She suspected Peel of trying to infiltrate Tory ladies into her Court circle, which was true enough because he insisted that too many of the so-named Ladies of the Bedchamber were Whigs. These were not dressers and hairbrushers. They were ladies who advised and even influenced the sovereign. Peel was right to think they were Whig wives. Melbourne stayed with Victoria until she discarded him when it was agreed she should marry Albert, the son of the Duke of Saxe-Coburg-Gotha.

It was not a very long marriage (1840–61), but clearly a healthy one. They had nine children, forty-two grandchildren and eighty-seven great-grandchildren. Victoria was thus related to almost every royal family in continental Europe and by the end of the nineteenth century was thought of as the grandmother of European royalty. She was, too, perhaps most famously, the first British Empress. She was created Empress of India in 1876. When we speak of the British Empire, we are strictly describing the possessions in the Indian subcontinent. The other lands under the Union Jack are colonies, dominions or dependencies. Yet the title 'empire' sits easily enough; by the end of Victoria's reign in 1901, about a quarter of the world's population was ruled by Britain and Victoria was sovereign of some four hundred and forty million people from more than fifty nations—about the same as the population of modern Europe.

As her ceremonial powers were extended, so the direct power of the monarchy was reduced. Would she, for example, have triumphed as she partly did in another bedchamber crisis? Probably not. Yet she did turn down Salisbury's suggestion that the Marquess of Lincolnshire should go as viceroy to India. Salisbury did not much argue the point either. It was the political power that was removed until she had little more than the right to be consulted, encourage and warn, as Walter Bagehot put it.[3] That was the political theorist's view in 1867. It would be his view of the powers of the British monarch in 2013.

After Victoria's death in 1901, the Prince of Wales became Edward VII, was followed by George V, who was followed briefly by Edward VIII, and then came George VI and Elizabeth. Of the five monarchs since 1901, Edward VIII is clearly the most interesting not because of what he did, but the manner of his going. The 1772 Royal Marriages Act required a member of the royal family to seek the sovereign's permission and therefore approval to marry. In his case, Edward VIII was the sovereign. His father and mother, King George V and Queen Mary of

---

[3] Walter Bagehot (1826–77) was the economist and political theorist of the time, whose 1867 *The English Constitution* is still used as a parliamentary reference.

Three kings in 1936—George V, Edward VIII and George VI. Edward
was forced to abdicate by the power of the Church of England, led by
Archbishop Cosmo Lang and Prime Minister Stanley Baldwin.

Teck, had refused to meet Wallis Simpson. Queen Mary, still alive when
Edward was king, had not changed her view. It was, however, a coali-
tion of the state Church of England's Archbishop of Canterbury, Cosmo
Lang, and the national government's Conservative Prime Minister,
Stanley Baldwin, that was behind the uncrowned king's abdication in
December 1936. The social authority, as well as the theological and
political understanding of these institutions, preordained these two
men's positions. Baldwin's crucial power was to threaten to resign if the
monarch did not give way. The last time that had happened was with
Pitt the Younger's threat to resign if George III did not give way over
Catholic emancipation in Ireland. The king would not. Pitt went.

In the approaching winter of 1936, the king gave way. That, by any
standard of change in the relationship between monarch and government, was a defining moment. The monarchy was confirmed as a
vulnerable institution that had few constitutional grounds once it
stepped outside the bounds of what government and then, at least, the
Church considered reasonable for the country.

Since the moment of Edward VIII's going, the British monarchy has had no constitutional and certainly no political place in British society. However, approaching the end of the line of more than fifty monarchs since Athelstan, Queen Elizabeth II is certainly unique in one respect. She has created the royal family. 'Royal family' is a semi-official title and only the Queen decides its members. Yet it is something other than an inner club. It is a very real family unit and sadly reflects not only the pleasanter side of the nation's identity. The royal family commonly offers a dysfunctional image. Of the Queen's four children, only one, Prince Edward, has a marriage that has survived. There is another aspect to this title. It is as if it were a family firm with working partners keeping it going. The Queen is the chair, or senior partner. In its more than thousand-year history the monarchy did not until Elizabeth II's reign *have* a working royal family. Having one now provides the basis for the next sovereign to carry the monarchy into the future.

Times Present

CHAPTER NINE

Royal Privilege and Duty

T he modern image of the Queen and the princes and princesses who stand either side of the sovereign on her constitutional balcony should not represent any social, even moral contradictions. Today the royalist and republican argue the principle of monarchy: hereditary position versus short-term elected leader. The former accepts monarchy as powerless celebrity. The latter's argument faces general indifference, because the sovereign has no power that cannot be usurped. The differences are irreconcilable, yet both tacitly accept the spectacle of the first family. As an example, the American first family is usually voted in by a small majority: as a very rough guide, fifty-one per cent of the nation supports it politically. However, apolitically, the US President and family rate in the high sixties, sometimes into the eighties. Galup, in 2012, showed Michelle Obama's rating at 66 per cent approval, whereas her husband's political rating was 52 per cent. The British monarch as a celebrity photo-opportunity, especially the royal balcony scene full of uniforms and waving, has about the same.

For the republican, a presidential head of state has a considerable and international workload and, other than in dictatorial examples, will be replaced by a popular vote after a short period. None would argue that a modern British monarch has the responsibilities of a political leader and even the oft-quoted experience of the present monarch being able to advise a Prime Minister or the Privy Council is somewhat far-fetched. Even if the Queen has seen it all before, even if a Prime Minister leaves a weekly audience at Buckingham Palace thoughtful of what the monarch may have said, the *Realpolitik* on returning to the Cabinet Room is a reminder that, contrary to what some would care to believe, the Queen has no role in the governing of the United Kingdom and the ruling party's international responsibilities.

Today, royalty's main value is reflecting a nation's identity, continuing to be the biggest brand name in the world, being a successful celebrity, delighting thousands on going about the business of being royal among people who rarely see anything but ordinariness. One royal visit to a school will live for a decade or more in the history of that establishment and a lifetime among the people, especially the children who were there. Royalty is wonderland among the people, never more so than when the tiara sparkles and the presence is a never-disappointing aura. Looking through opinion polling to assess how that plays out in most British lives, we must first glance at relevant facts and figures: how many visits does the Queen make each year? How many hours does she work each day and doing what? Where does she get money from?

In 1697, Parliament passed the Civil List Act to pay for the running of government and authorised the patronages of the monarch. That worked for a time, but as the business of monarchy became more expensive, another and more consistent means had to be found to fund the crown. In 1761 George III agreed to give up all the rents and other payments from crown lands in return for Parliament giving him an annual sum—a living allowance. That Act was amended in 1831 so that the payments did not include government expenses. It is not unreasonable to choose that moment as the point when government and monarchy separated. Seventy years later, in 1901, further payments were made into the Civil List to meet the costs of other members of the royal family. Post-Diana opinion polls suggested a new mood among royalists: even they wondered why the taxpayer should be picking up the bills of often not very popular members of royalty.

In 2012, at the end of the tax year, the system changed. Instead of the Civil List and the grants-in-aid for the upkeep of the palaces, travel and public relations and information, Parliament agreed to five-yearly funding, called the Sovereign Grant. It is not much more than an accountancy job, with the review being carried out by the Prime Minister and Chancellor of the Exchequer of the day and the Queen's Keeper of the Privy Purse, her finance director. The Privy Purse is the private purse, the Queen's personal and private income. It comes largely from the Duchy of Lancaster (as opposed to Prince Charles's income, which comes from the Duchy of Cornwall), a forty-six-thousand-acre estate belonging through trusts to the monarch since it was created for John of Gaunt. It has been the monarch's trust land since 1399 and the reign of Bolingbroke as Henry IV. It is valued at some £350 million, and the sovereign gets the profits from rentals and trade on the Duchy, and pays income tax on them. To keep an eye on the accounting, the House of Commons Public Accounts Select Committee and the National Audit Office take evidence on the workings of the bookkeeping of the royal household. The household is a larger office than may be thought, as it is rarely reviewed. There are five offices based at Buckingham Palace: the Private Secretary, the Master of the Household, the Lord Chamberlain, the Treasurer and the Keeper of the Privy Purse. Between them, they employ around 1,200 people, some 450 of whom are paid for by the taxpayer. They are all there to keep the institution of monarchy in working order. The centrepiece, the sovereign, has a routine that relies on everything being at hand and few decisions that are not anticipated by the levels of staffing.

A typical day begins with newspaper headlines followed by a selection of the three hundred or so letters addressed to her on any one day, most of which can be answered by staff who understand what the Queen would expect to be said in the reply. Others she will deal with herself. Replies are never long; little time is spent on them. The first 'must-do' list of the day follows with two private secretaries going through state and Cabinet papers, and official documents. The secretaries make sure the answers to likely questions from the Queen are at hand.

A lot of that session is taken up with understanding and signing, but never the latter before the former, and many of the papers have been read by the Queen in the late hours of the previous evening. Unless there are scheduled excursions, much of the morning is then devoted to official visitors, including British diplomats on the move. Each gets about twenty minutes. All this is completed by 11 am. That is the hour set apart for investitures, although others, including the Prince of

Wales, take on some of those duties. Lunch usually means guests and the afternoons are taken up with one or more of the three hundred or so public engagements a year. When there are no official dinners or outings, the monarch will, each Wednesday and without notes, meet the Prime Minister privately. But this is not the only political session. Every evening when Parliament is sitting, the Whips' office sends a report of the day's proceedings and this is read, not skimmed.

If this seems a gruelling schedule—visits, trips, state papers, more than ninety thousand letters and between three and four hundred engagements a year, including political and set pieces such as investitures, and sometimes having three complete changes of clothes from morning until the formality of a banquet—it might be remembered that on any one day there are in the royal household more than a thousand people to make everything work wherever the Queen is on whatever day. This applies also when the royal family goes on holiday. Putting those three hundred or so engagements in context, we can add the luxury of six weeks' Christmas holiday at Sandringham and the summer break at Balmoral (although there are still duties, and red boxes to go through, on holiday), all of which makes a workload easier to carry. There is no doubt that the sovereign works hard; equally, the palace and household staff represent all that is efficient in royal bureaucracy and the monarch's task is much easier for it. Moreover, there is often an image presented of the Queen as an untiring and selfless sovereign with enviable stamina. Long holidays and seemingly tireless and efficient staff ease the burdens of the day to day tasks of the Queen.

The public image of the monarch is professionally presented by one of the more efficient public relations systems in any royal family worldwide. It is one of steady industry and duty on behalf of the country and her people without the luxury of speaking too pointedly, although there are ways for a modern monarch to make sure royal feelings are understood. Nevertheless, it must remain an example of modern British monarchy that during her more than sixty years on the throne, the Queen has barely uttered anything memorable. For the public, there are Maundy Money ceremonies, delight at Royal Ascot, impeccably dressed visits, ceremonials at Garter processions and the opening of Parliament, and a voice expressed in a written script, one almost never heard in casual conversation which might otherwise give a clue as to the person who is monarch. During great events, generously cheerful or, more rarely, inexpressibly tragic, the public can only say what it thinks of the nation's longest surviving institution and its steward when responding to carefully crafted questions that elicit that most dangerous response of a nation: public opinion.

CHAPTER TEN

Diana and the Pollsters

S hortly before the death of Diana, Princess of Wales, in the summer of 1997, Ipsos MORI had polled six hundred adults over the age of eighteen to test the mood under the new government of Tony Blair and feelings on key issues with the royal family. There is little good research on how a liked or disliked government influences public moods towards royalty, but anecdotal evidence suggests that a popular Prime Minister can have considerable influence on public opinion of the major institutions, including the monarchy. The Prime Minister's relationship with the monarch is one for clever or gossipy analysis; neither may necessarily be wrong. This has been true since the first Prime Minister, Robert Walpole, and his relationship with George I, Pitt the Younger's with George III, Melbourne's, Peel's, Disraeli's and Gladstone's with Victoria, Baldwin's with Edward VIII, and most certainly Churchill's, Margaret Thatcher's and Tony Blair's with Elizabeth II.

There was something approaching public glee at the thought that the Queen might disapprove of both Margaret Thatcher and Tony Blair. The sense of how these Prime Ministers approached the monarchy had some bearing on the public opinion of each. For all the system of democracy, the public—for reasons not always explicable, never mind explained— seems to think the Prime Minister is wished upon them, whereas the Queen has almost nothing to do with a democratic option. The standing of the Prime Minister in crisis is an obvious impediment to public acceptance of his or her solutions; stand that doubt alongside a national mood involving the royal family and it is easy to see why opinion poll soundings become of utmost importance. The ratings of monarch and politician become entwined. So it was in early August 1997.

In the summer of 1997, Tony Blair had a seventy per cent approval rating, his government fifty-four per cent; a complex set of figures suggested that the public had no immediate need to judge the government's performance. It had been in power only since the spring. There were no major issues that questioned the electorate's decision to give Blair a huge majority and it could have been that the public had had enough of politics for the moment. That PM-monarchy equation was clearly seen in the question about abolition. Half the country thought it would be worse off without the Queen or a king and the continuing average was shown again that about a third thought the monarchy or lack of it would make no difference to the nation's fortunes. Furthermore, the vast majority of the people, some eighty per cent, thought that the monarchy would still be around in ten years, although only thirty-five per cent thought it would survive the average polled person's remaining lifetime: for maybe another fifty years.

As for individual royals, Prince Charles did not get good notices. Forty-six per cent thought he was not very good at his job. It is not surprising that about the same number thought he should step aside in the line of accession and that Prince William should be his grandmother's heir. It was inevitable that when the people were asked which three members of the royal family had most damaged its reputation, the public said Charles first, followed by the Duchess of York, Sarah Ferguson, and then Diana, Princess of Wales.

The year 1997, was said to be a good-mood year and one of hope. The long-serving Conservatives had been discarded by the electorate and the country was now led by Tony Blair, who promised much, including what was called New Labour and the promise that his party was not a party of envy bent on ruling Britain under Labour's constitutional shibboleth, Clause 4, within which almost anything could be taken into state ownership for the common wealth.

Most significantly in the mood swing of the popularity of the royal family was the death of Diana. Quick reaction to an event-polling is difficult to assess. The survey immediately after an event produces answers influenced by the time; responses twelve months later must allow for memory, and the personal feelings and influences on the person answering the same question. Interestingly, the answers—a year apart—may not be different. These are the difficulties of judging opinion research.

For our purpose, with the circumstances surrounding Diana still news items and therefore hard to ignore, there were four opinions that would reflect the relationship between the royal family, the public and the media: public feelings towards the Queen and her heir, Prince Charles; the position of the monarchy in British life; the media and the monarchy; and the way in which the media 'lived' off the death of Diana for twelve months.

The view of how good a job the Queen and the Prince of Wales were doing suggested a recovery of public admiration for the family or maybe that the media had misjudged the mood and, looking for somewhere to take the Diana story, had overplayed the reaction of the royal family. Twelve months after Diana's death, seventy-three per cent of those polled said they were satisfied that the Queen was doing a good job and sixty-three per cent thought Prince Charles was also doing well. Moreover, these figures explained the answers to questions about the monarchy itself. More than half of the people thought the country would be worse off without a monarchy and twenty-nine per cent thought it would make no difference if the UK became a republic.

On the media coverage of the royals, opinion was reasonably split; thirty-three per cent thought the media gave too much coverage to them and the same number thought the balance was about right. The surprise for editors was in the columns that questioned the number of Diana stories in papers, magazines and broadcast media. Sixty-three per cent thought the media had got it wrong and had given 'much too much' coverage to the continuing speculation about Diana's death and its consequences.

Two years on, attention had turned from the late Diana to the position and image of the then Camilla Parker Bowles. Mrs Parker Bowles and her husband of twenty-two years had divorced in 1995. Her affair with the Prince of Wales had been known for some time by her husband and by the Queen. Mrs Parker Bowles had long been the woman in the life of Prince Charles, and anecdotally was the 'other woman' and one of the causes of the Charles-Diana divorce. An irony of that relationship was that many in royal circles still believe that Mrs Parker Bowles selected, certainly approved, Diana as a suitable bride for Charles.

The Charles-Camilla publicity did not turn people away from modern monarchy. A poll published in June 1999 suggested that two-thirds of those polled still appeared to believe that the monarch had an important role and, further, seventy-four per cent favoured Britain remaining a monarchy.[1] Almost two years after Diana's death, Ipsos MORI reported that almost two-thirds of those questioned were comfortable with the Charles-Camilla friendship and thought the couple should remain together, that Mrs Parker Bowles should appear at public engagements with the Prince of Wales and that she should spend time with the young princes, William and Harry.

However, much behind these answers could be interpreted as coming from a British society that by the late 1990s had no strong and certainly no religious feelings about the rights and wrongs of divorce and new relationships. In 1999, for example, there were 263,000 marriages in Britain and more than 144,000 divorces.[2] The distinction between 'moral' and constitutional values, again anecdotal, appeared marked when the public thought it was one thing for Charles to marry Camilla, but quite another for her to become queen. Fifty-nine per cent thought it was perfectly fine for Charles to be king should he be married to Mrs Parker Bowles (whom the Queen at that time had not officially met as his 'partner'). However, when people were asked the direct question, Do you think Camilla should become Queen at his side?, the answer was an emphatic majority 'no'. Seventy-six per cent of the poll said Camilla could be married to Charles, but certainly not be queen. Why should there have been a difference between what was fine, morally, and what was the unquestionable form of who sits on the throne?

Mrs Parker Bowles was still very much portrayed by the media (and it was therefore the only image for the general public) as a royal mistress, not the easiest image in a society imbued with Thatcherite 'self' and thus double standards when comparing how the people in the street behaved

[1] Ipsos MORI, published in the *Sun* on 18 June 1999 with the theme 'Royal Family and the Monarchy'.
[2] Office of National Statistics, 2000.

compared with what was now expected of royalty. The Diana phenom-
enon rested uneasily in the judgemental attitudes of the public. Prince
Charles was still, by and large, less than admired and so Mrs Parker
Bowles might never be able to shake off the 'mistress' reputation, maybe
even after they were married. An ancestor of hers had been a mistress of
Edward VII and that, while not quite common knowledge, did nothing
to help the Camilla cause. For the British, there was no precedence of
mistresses or lovers becoming queen or king or consorts—prince consort
or princess consort. It was one thing to take tea together, another to sit
side by side regaled, enthroned and crowned. Public opinion appeared
constant. MORI suggested in early August 1997 that some thirty-four
per cent thought the couple should continue their relationship, but not
flaunt it. They should keep private their feelings and closeness. A year
later, the figure was more or less the same: thirty-five per cent. In 1999,
the figure was thirty-three per cent. In the same period, forty-eight per
cent said they should be open about their relationship.

These attitudes towards monarchy and the individuals in the Palace
were relatively consistent with expectations that influenced answers when
there were major events or even crises. For example, if we accept at least
some truth in the notion offered earlier that monarchy reflects the identity of the people, we have also to consider that identity in terms of how
the people see themselves or, if we can ever find such a passing mood,
how the people are touched by an event beyond the event itself. If there is
a dramatic change in government, as there was in 1979 when the United
Kingdom elected its first woman Prime Minister, or an event so unexpected
and directly reflecting the behaviour of royalty as on 31 August 1997, when
Diana was killed. The common misunderstanding lies within the single
rather than the multiple reading of focus groups and opinion polls.

How people polled in the south-east are touched by an event may not
be how those living in, say, the north-east are touched. Moreover, the
effect may not be as long-lasting as imagined. For example, middle-aged
and middle-class women tend to be supportive of Prince Charles because
they are in his generation range and were enthralled by him as the
young prince. More complex analysis is in the sympathies in those same
female groups towards his married life, especially with many in uneasy
marriages, and some possibly in affairs and others in second marriages.
The questions put to the public about Prince Charles could tell us more

about social reactions than general opinion. This is certainly true when younger audiences—fifteen to twenty-five-year-olds—are quizzed. Any idea that the young are against monarchy should be re-examined. There is some evidence that the younger groupings are more pro-monarchy than the older ones.

In the second half of July 2001 a poll was carried out by Market & Opinion Research International in conjunction with a MORI survey for *Reader's Digest*.[3] A third believed Britain would be better off without a monarchy, but more than half (about fifty-four per cent) wanted to keep royalty. Furthermore, this generation was confident enough to believe in its influence and an average of three-quarters of those polled thought the monarchy would survive another five years. That was hardly a remarkable prediction, although some thought might be given to the fact that five years was a third of the lifetime of part of the group. When asked the same question, whether Britain would or would not have a monarchy in fifty years (for many of them, their expected remaining life expectancy), more than half said that within fifty years Britain would not have a monarchy. It should be said that half the country might also think that few institutions would survive for another half-century.

The first decade of the twenty-first century saw perhaps more changes in the ways of life in British society than had taken place during the whole period since the end of the Second World War. The changes could be generationally alienating, for example with advances in personal computers and telephones. A generation that could cope with the simplest laptops and phones was struggling to learn the world of apps. Why would fast changes touch perceptions of monarchy? Part of the response lies in identity. Identity is assumed or a dawning of what or whom a person and collectively a nation of people are. The bombardment of possibilities in mobiles and tablets usurped the recognised process of identity. Identity is predictable; it reflects status, background, social and economic position. For the majority, that status, thus identity, was inescapable. Modern IT ignores those restrictions. It puts the individual in touch with possibilities never before imagined. It offers access to a different level of identity

---

[3] Between 19 and 31 July 2001, 645 people between fifteen and twenty-five were interviewed at home and face to face.

and one that can be changed almost at will. With one touch of a screen IT language could move an ordinary person quickly among the possibilities and the illusion of being in some sort of control of that transition. With this social movement came the suspicions that it was now clear that cherished institutions carried false identities, and that geekism had replaced the sure-footed way to financial and commercial authority. Once that perception was in general acceptance, there arrived an indifference to the great institutions: the Church of England, banking, politics and the monarchy. It meant that hallowed institutional images were no longer important. That indifference did not mean opposition; indifference alone was far more destructive.

By the spring of 2002 a series of polls suggested that eighty per cent of the country wanted to stay under the system of constitutional monarchy and slightly more than forty per cent felt that if anything the monarchy was stronger than it had been in a very long time, but there was no indication that the nation was particularly supportive of monarchy, only that it liked it. Indifference weakened the easy transfer from like to support, surprisingly so when the chairman of MORI, Professor Sir Robert Worcester, said that these indicated some of the healthiest ratings for the royal family in some twenty years, 'with some of the highest ratings we have monitored for the Queen in the last two decades'.[4] Ten years on, during the Queen's Jubilee year, the public's affection for the royal family was at a zenith. In June 2012, the Queen's personal standing was, as may have been expected, the highest ever since polling started on her personal rating.[5]

Ninety per cent of British adults said they were satisfied with the way in which the Queen carried out her role. Given the conditions of the country, especially the constant economic pressures, it might be no surprise that the Queen's rating was higher than the combined rating of the Prime Minister, David Cameron (thirty-four per cent), and that of the leader of Her Majesty's Opposition, Ed Miliband (thirty-five per cent), neither of whom are in jobs likely to inspire the public affection in a society with little sense

[4] 30 May 2002 commenting on poll results by Ipsos MORI for Granada Media and ITV1's *Tonight with Trevor MacDonald*.
[5] 1992.

of contemporary history—and that believed Winston Churchill was the last in Downing Street so to do. This was a year of grand celebration, and of the London Olympics, so the figure would reflect general good feeling, unlike the post-Diana ratings of sixty-six per cent.

Second-in-line for public plaudit was not the heir to the throne Prince Charles, but the one after, Prince William. He had the same nine-out-of-ten people saying 'well done', as they said of his grandmother. Among the younger population the eighteen to thirty-four group, his MORI polling figures were even higher, and not surprisingly. Yet a third from that same age group, although in great support of Wills and Kate, did not support the monarchy as an institution, whereas only thirteen per cent of an older generation, the fifty-five year olds and above, felt the same way. The younger voter, with no constitutional understanding it seems, gave the impression that it would make better sense if William and not his father followed his grandmother to the throne.

Prince Charles was, according to the Fleet Street royal watchers, not quite delighted by the media adoration of his son and daughter-in-law over himself and Camilla, especially as polling suggested seventy-eight per cent thought Charles was doing a fine job—a long way up from the polling in 1997 when his rating was only four out of ten. More importantly for the Palace image-makers, those people suggesting he should step aside for William were the lowest in a decade. Slightly fewer than thirty-six per cent thought he should not be king. Constitutionally, Prince Charles could abdicate as heir if he thought it best to do so, or if, for example, there had been some difficulty over his marriage plans as there had been for Edward VIII. Nothing like that was contemplated. Under normal circum-stances he would have to be incapacitated before William could take over his role, although not his title. As in an earlier age, the next-in-line would then 'rule' as regent. Nothing in public opinion has strongly reflected the idea of jumping generations, and whatever the variations in opinion the numbers have evened out during the past twenty years or so.

The polling figures over a decade reflected constants, such as the popu-larity of the Queen, if not always the same popularity for the monarchy. A further caution had to be the fickleness in opinion that could reflect a tendency for those questioned never to have thought seriously about the subject; when confronted by a pollster, a person might easily feel he or she was not quite sure what they thought about the question and hurried into a reply. There was the last resort of someone telling an untruth to the polling team either out of mischief or because he or she did not want to be seen giving what at the time might have been considered to be the 'wrong' answer. Some would have speculated that Prince Charles, of all the members of the royal family, could be a victim of this fickle answering. In November 2012, during a year in which the heir to the throne appeared increasingly irrelevant during royal occasions, the prince's rating declined to just twenty-one per cent. Pollsters suggested Prince Charles was showing an almost fifty-per-cent ratings decline since what royal watchers perceived as a PR offensive in 2012.

Moreover, only a variable and barely measurable two per cent thought his wife, the Duchess of Cornwall, was at all popular. That was a low figure, by any measure in polling numbers. Nor should it have been influenced by the seemingly continuing question over the status of Camilla should her husband become king. The question of whether she will be known as Queen Camilla was set aside in a statement on Prince Charles's website that year: 'As was explained at the time of their wedding in April 2005, it is intended that The Duchess will be known as HRH The Princess Consort when The Prince of Wales accedes to The Throne'. Polling in 2012 before Parliament's consideration of royal succession[6] showed that Charles had dropped in popularity, while Prince William was even more popular than the Queen:

Prince William	62
The Queen	48
Prince Harry	36
Duchess of Cambridge	23
Prince Charles	21
Princess Anne	14
Prince Philip	11
Prince Andrew	2
Duchess of Cornwall	2
Prince Edward	1
None liked	5

[6] King's College, University of London/Ipsos MORI, 2012.

William's popularity is not a surprise to pollsters using the younger generations (nineteen to thirty-five year olds). The wedding of Prince William and Kate Middleton had a fairytale image. Prince William said that he wanted the wedding to be the 'people's wedding'. The imagery of young, physically attractive knights and ladies from a modern Camelot could easily inspire envy and even antagonism among those with very little in a society that sometimes does not listen to the anxieties of those without, other than to foster an undertone of annoyance that the disadvantaged are on benefits and so stealing from the state. That is the one undeniable extreme. It is true also that the disadvantaged are rarely questioned by opinion pollsters. The extremes of society are not trusted in any debate, even in the sophisticated system of modern polling. The views of those people are rarely heard and when they are they are too easily categorised as predictable for their sort.

There is another side that those figures tie in with; the author carried out unscientific polling, using three questions among just two hundred people over three months. This time the spread contradicted most polling rules that want to know what people feel on a specific day

William the Last?—Prince William on his wedding day,
a significant moment in his popularity ratings

with similar circumstances influencing answers. The questioning began
in January 2013 and was carried out on each Thursday by random
telephone calling, stopping-and-asking strangers in London train
stations and casual conversations. The object was to see how low-key
opinion-gathering compared with the more trustworthy forms used by
established polling organisations. The sample was taken from thirty-
somethings to early sixty-year-olds and the questions were deliberately
tabloid in nature to test bar-talk reactions. Who are your top five
royals? Which royal would you be happiest with replacing the Queen?
Do you want the monarchy to be here for the rest of your life?

Who are your top five royals?

Queen	121
Prince Harry	29
Prince Philip	21
William	18
Princess Anne	11

Which royal would you be happiest with replacing the Queen?

Prince William	83
Prince Philip	60
Prince Charles	51
Don't care	6

Do you want the monarchy to be here for the rest of your life?

Yes	115
Don't mind	58
No	27

The major change in the response as shown in the very much more
organised London University/Ipsos MORI on p. 133 was the popularity
of Prince Philip. There could be two reasons for his popularity jump
from a relatively low position where his unique constitutional position allows him to be a celebrity within the royal family, but to have no
hereditary role and never to be a factor in the succession debate or even

in the discussion about the monarchy. His position echoes his disgruntlement in the early years of the Queen's reign. When discovering he had nothing to do unless he created work for himself, he is said to have remarked that he was 'nothing but a bloody amoeba'.

The first reason for his rise in the polls was the 2012 Jubilee. The polling took place at the end of that year during which Prince Philip was very prominent and on public view as much as the Queen. By then, his popularity standing was fifty-eight per cent—eleven points up since the start of the year. Second, this was a time when Prince Philip was in hospital; given his age, there was strong media attention on his chances of survival and he was sympathetically covered rather than subjected to the usual journalistic line that searches for yet another Duke-of-Edinburgh gaff. In short, the prince was noticed more and evidence of the way in which the Queen relied on him was obvious.

Constitutionally, there would be absolutely no possibility in any circumstances of Prince Philip succeeding to the throne. He is not even prince consort. Prince Charles is next-in-line and that is the end of it, constitutionally. It may be that there is a mood that would have Prince William on the throne before his father. As we stand, there is no possibility of that. Now that the prince also has an heir and therefore the nation, everything is settled. Yet the public often does not ask for a constitutional expectation. It picks up a mood and expresses it. The important factor here is that there is no anecdotal or polling evidence to suggest that the mood is important to the public. So certain are the majority of the British in the ways of monarchy and particularly influenced by their experience of the Queen that the succession is, as Westminster politicians describe it, nothing but good-natured tea-room talk. In other words, the British are confident that they have the right monarchy and the system has no need to change. Yet that system may change for reasons hardly imagined and certainly not thought through by the people over whom the British monarch reigns. Events and moods will have their influence, though few imagine them now.

The most obvious event-mood combination for pondering the future of the monarchy will arrive as one reign draws to a close and is seen as doing so. Age has the final say in most lives. The age of the monarch begins to have a say in the mood of the nation and its identity.

CHAPTER ELEVEN

The 1940s to Today

W ill Prince George ever be king? Can we have any idea what form of monarchy will exist in, say, fifty or sixty years' time when a canny actuary would suggest the throne may be vacant for him? Everything that we have covered thus far, from Celtic princes to statehood to kingship to the development of monarchy into a rich, internationally political and military power, gives us the background to provide a context for certain questions. Very simply, will Britain remain a monarchy? If not, what will bring it to an end and if it continues what will it look like? We can start with yet another obvious statement: the constitutional crystal ball clears as the present reign draws to a close.

A dead monarch takes away the style of monarchy. In the second decade of the twenty-first century, there are few who remember times under George VI. His period, from the 1930s to the austerity of the early 1950s, is recorded, studied and restudied, but little is understood of what it was like to have George VI as king, particularly as much of his reign was in wartime, which is when all leadership, even kingly, has a distorted image. He ruled for just twelve years, five of which (May 1940 to July 1945) were dominated by the leadership figure of Winston Churchill.

The monarchy of that time, even though Britain took a pasting in a worldwide war, was necessarily remote. The image was of a caring but unknowing monarchy, dressed mostly as an admiral in the rubble of blitzed London. There was no twenty-four-hour television to enhance and explain the image; indeed, there were few televisions and the war-suspended service meant there were no television programmes until the BBC was reopened in 1948 to cover the London Olympics. Newspaper and magazine coverage of the royal family was mostly in features, and reporting was very respectful of the monarch and its order of things. Certainly there was no social media—only about ten per cent of the population had access to an indoor telephone and this included those in offices; when a household did have a phone, it was often shared with another house, a party line. In the year Prince Charles was born, 1948, all new telephone subscribers had to share a line with someone else. Evening queues at the United Kingdom's 52,000 phone-boxes were unremarkable aspects of British life. In spite of the social and polit-ical revolution of George VI's time, this was also a society that knew its place in the social order. The images of class distinctions, economi-cally designed as well as those of birthright and inheritance at the other end of the social scale, were clearly drawn. First names were for the lower and working classes. Surnames were familiarities of the upper-middle classes and above. This author's father, who had met George VI, remarked that royalty even 'smelled differently, like no smell I'd ever come across. It was an old smell.' If nothing else, Palace talcs and soaps set aside the aristocracy and were as mysterious as the people them-selves. This illustration is not as far-fetched as it might seem, for this was an age when the majority of the population still lived cheaply and ordinarily, and the social distinctions of custom and relation were yet to be torn at by the revolution of late-1950s Britain and in the 1960s, when conscription disappeared along with the short-back-and sides and the mental images that went with that generation.

There were two further reasons why the British public would never have had a remarkable view on what it should think of the monarch and the monarchy's future. First, in George VI's reign a nation that had been to war would hardly think about how it might be ruled in future. Second, apart from the circumstances that brought about the reign of George VI, there was nothing out of the ordinary about it. Within two years of becoming king, George VI announced his country was at war with Germany and within a year the baton of personality war leadership was handed to Churchill. Apart from a few appearances, the king was not required to do much, but there was a feeling that it was good that he and Queen Elizabeth were there. In 1947, the spirits were lifted by the marriage of a princess and a handsome prince in naval uniform. The country was far from innocent, but the royal family did nothing to disturb the peace. When the king died, the country was ready for a new Elizabethan age. It arrived at exactly the right time. Even sugar was no longer rationed; Stalin died; and men climbed the world's highest mountain.

Thus the reign of Elizabeth II opened with a peel of hope. Sixty years later, that relationship with the monarch has not changed. The Queen has not changed. She has aged and is eighty-seven in 2013. Monarchs are not invulnerable, but monarchs age like good cottage gardens; mostly, they give greater pleasure. Moreover, in Queen Elizabeth's case there is an image of the reliability of someone hardly known or under-stood by her people and at a constant distance from them. She has uttered barely a memorable sentence; most of her people have wanted it that way. It has always been best for a monarch to be seen but rarely heard. Anecdotally and through the opinion polls, the public has never wanted to contradict the concept of monarchy, so it has been best that that same public has only been aware of the image rather than the person who reigns over them.

Most obviously, the monarch's feelings—apart from those towards her winners at Ascot or hidden by very expressionless stares in private—are not publicly known. Disapproval of major issues or personalities can hardly be pinned down. Former servants, high-blown or not, do not tell much. The most famous so-called revelation came when Marion Crawford (1909–88), the former nanny to then Princesses Elizabeth and Margaret, and called 'Crawfie' by Margaret, told all in 1950 in her book, *The Little Princesses: The Story of the Queen's Childhood by her Nanny*. Crawfie was sent packing and neither Elizabeth nor Margaret spoke of or to her again. The stories that do emerge are anecdotal telltales or might as well be because they are never confirmed with any authority and are soon forgotten by the public who do not much care, unless the story has been about Diana. Gossip is gossip: fascinating, but it remains gossip.

In short, in spite of three or four meetings with outsiders in a

single day, and sixty years of televised visits and tours, dinners, luncheons and investitures, and in spite of being the single most long-term
recognisable person in the world, Elizabeth II remains to most of her
subjects an enigma. The manner of her coming to the throne has something to do with that. On Wednesday, 6 February 1952, Elizabeth heard
the news of King George VI's death and so became queen at the age of
twenty-five and crowned a year later on 2 June 1953. Her very public
life before that was perhaps no more than seven years—delightful,
but little known and none of it too gossipy or, let it be said, very interesting, another asset for a queen who has never upset or disturbed her
subjects. Her subjects have never had to much think, if at all, about
whether monarchy is right for modern Britain. Here, then, the change
for the future for a new monarch can and, in Charles's case, will excite
fresh thoughts.

The successor, familiar as a celebrity, assumes a different image once
Saint Edward's crown has settled. After the accession the king becomes
as visible as the old sovereign; but in spite of perhaps decades as king-
in-waiting and after the initial celebrations, it takes time for the public
to know what it really thinks of the new sovereign while the king has
presumably long made up his mind about what he thinks of his people;
the people of course may never know. Thus, once great events are left
behind, the function of monarchy is more than the personality and
reflection of his or her nation's identity.

Anticipating the effectiveness of and public support for a new
monarch is not a matter of having a preconception and judgement of the
heir during the monarch's reign. Prince Charles is not an exceptional
case of the heir to the throne having mixed previews, especially from
the media. The Japanese wondered—but rarely aloud—before the death
of Emperor Hirohito in 1989 if the then crown prince, Akihito, would
be as benign as his father was once he occupied the Chrysanthemum
Throne as Japan's 125th ruler. If he did find this difficult Akihito
expressed no thoughts on the matter; nor did he need to. He did what
Japanese emperors had done for centuries. He remained remote and
therefore an enigma, so much so that it was not until the trauma in
March 2011 of the tsunami and earthquake that he even spoke to the
Japanese nation at all (with a television and radio broadcast for calm),

other than his annual 23 December birthday address, not unlike the Queen's Christmas broadcast.

Because there is now an electronic message board in the form of social media, there is also for the first time a tempting platform for those who question the need for the world's oldest surviving monarchy. There are plenty of discussions on Japanese websites that inspire the same reaction: the emperor is the known and only reliable element in Japanese society that can and does rise above mistrust of the political elite. Given the difficulties in Japanese public life, natural and particularly man-made, it is little wonder that the Japanese turn to a figure—until the 1940s believed to be god-like—for the surest motto and encouragement for national identity: 'Do not lose hope'.

Monarchs do not give speeches, except on notable occasions. Therefore they are listened to with something approaching an intensity of a nation wanting to believe what is said. That is a further difference between political and hereditary leadership. It is, too, in a continuous communication age, a never-to-be-dismissed expression of the people seemingly having made up their minds, or rarely hiding their concerns, of what and who will follow their present monarch. Akihito understood this and the Japanese system preserved the protocol of distance. Could there be a lesson for the British monarchy? There is no evidence sustaining the feeling that constitutional democracies need in the twenty-first century to be 'bicycling monarchies' to have the best function for the people.

Bicycling monarchies have no more value than a society wedding and can exist only in countries small enough not to have many easily, internationally recognised identities; and, of course, within democracies. Most importantly, when considering the future of monarchy at large and the United Kingdom's in particular, it is to be remembered that the majority of world monarchies, including each one in Europe, exist within free-voting democracies, which suggests a reason why monarchies may still be popular: they are wanted by free-voting peoples. Twenty-three per cent of all countries in the world have kings or queens. Of 192 states, more than forty are ruled by monarchies—a quarter of them by the same one: Elizabeth II. A couple of monarchies are eccentrically constitutional. Yet there are only six monarchs enthroned in undemocratic societies: the pope is *ex officio* sovereign of the Vatican.

More autocratically, there are five monarchies where the sovereign rules with absolute authority and where to challenge that usually dynastic right may be seen as an act of treason. The monarchs or sultans of Brunei, Oman, Qatar, Saudi Arabia and Swaziland are absolute rulers. The historical oddity may be Andorra, in which since the eighteenth century there has existed a diarchy—it has two monarchs, or more accurately princes, as it is a principality. The anomaly is that one of the princes is an office of the serving President of France; thus at the time of writing, François Hollande is constitutional *ex-officio* co-prince of Andorra and the other is Bishop Joan Enric Vives i Sicília, the Bishop of Urgell, the Roman Catholic diocese in Catalonia.

To compare monarchies as examples of the direction in which the British system may go, it is logical to compare thrones in similar democracies. Thus, continental Europe is the easier comparison and a region in which large parts were not, until the nineteenth century, in a territorial foundation that would be recognised today. It was a time, particularly after the Napoleonic ambition, truly to draw lines, although gradually rather than in any haste. A century ago, Europe was awash with monarchies; only France, San Marino and Switzerland were republics. By the close of the twentieth century most European states had elected heads of state, although constitutional sovereigns ruled in all remaining states, with the exception of the Vatican.[1]

Denmark is constitutionally the oldest unbroken monarchy in Europe, with origins in the tenth century, and is, according to opinion polls in Denmark, the most popular in Europe. In April 2010, more than eighty per cent of those polled wanted to continue with the monarchy, although half of those in support wanted to reduce even the token powers of the sovereign, such as appointing the Prime Minister, whereas a law needs the monarch's signature before it may be enacted.[2] In January 2012, thirty-nine years after Queen Margrethe became sovereign, figures suggested her popularity remained at around eighty per cent and that some sixteen per cent would prefer a republic.

---

[1] These states are Andorra, Belgium, Denmark, Liechtenstein, Luxembourg, Monaco, the Netherlands, Norway, Spain, Sweden and the United Kingdom.
[2] Ramboll Management/Analyse Denmark: 1009 people were polled between 1 and 4 March 2010.

According to Copenhagen University analysts, in all probability the continuing popularity had much to do with the steady rather than dramatic pace of modernisation in the royal family, popular marriages and the relatively low cost of maintaining the royal family: about €45 million a year. Could it all change? Most unlikely.

Across the bridge from Denmark, the Swedish view of monarchy makes for sometimes uncomfortable reading for royalists. King Carl XVI Gustaf is often accused of philandering and generally denies such accusations, but many Swedes wonder how they keep coming. Most polling recently notes that a majority of people questioned have lost faith in the monarchy and that the king's behaviour has been responsible for that loss in public confidence. The strength of opposition has been as high as sixty per cent. With a credibility warning, recent figures were published on behalf of the Swedish republican movement by the respected Novus Opinion, which polled twenty-eight per cent of Swedes preferring a president. In Sweden there is a retirement age of sixty-five and some Swedes say it should apply to the monarch. Could the crown fall? The answer is another 'not yet', because the fortunes of the monarchy's popularity could be in the hands of the king's very popular heir, Crown Princess Victoria, particularly after the recent birth of her daughter.

In the third of the Scandinavian states, Norway, the republican movement is more defined. In a 2009 poll for the national broadcaster, Norsk Rikskringkasting AS or NRK (the Norwegian Broadcasting Corporation), forty per cent of lawmakers wanted a republic. Why is this different from others in the region? First, the Norwegian Parliament has a powerful young generation of members, and this is supported by the NRK poll that claimed only fifty-six per cent want the royal family and that many think the change could come within two decades. The second reason for a slight anti-royal theme goes back a decade, to 2001, when the then Crown Prince Haakon married Mette-Marit Tjessem Høiby, who, or so it was claimed, was a member of Oslo's druggy partying group, as well as having a son from a previous relationship. Again, it is the personality and perception of individuals and not the institution that shifts public opinion. Could Norway lose its monarchy? Yes: it is the most vulnerable in Europe.

That might have been the case in Belgium, where a monarch, often ill-liked, has ruled since 1831. Until 2013, the national Belgian mood said, in effect, that Albert II was old, boring and distant.[3] In the summer of 2013, the seventy-nine-year-old king abdicated, saying that he was tired and it was time to go. He went with his country seemingly forever split between Dutch-speaking north and French-speaking south, and his son, Philippe, took the oath in Dutch, French and German. Belgium, not recognised as a place of celebrity until the past half-century when it became the centre of the European Union's government, has tested perhaps the only non-ceremonial duty of the monarch, the nation's constitutional management. The crown's support comes largely from among the people in French-language Wallonia. Dutch-speaking Flanders is far more anti-monarchy. The 2014 elections, at the time of writing, are expected to be a test of Belgium's constitutional identity, with separatists gaining influence. Will the monarch last much longer? More probably not than possibly yes. The country is divided, with Flanders seen as an active centre of separatism. A finally broken Belgium could not support an overall monarchy. If Dutch-speaking Flanders is seen as less than royalist, that mood has not spread next door, to Holland.

The Netherlands has been a recognisable state since the sixteenth century, although not in the instance seen today. Historically, as with other parts of continental Europe, Holland was a territory of split allegiances. In 1581, it became the Republic of the Seven United Netherlands and stuck as this until Napoleon. Under the French it was called, in 1795, the Batavian Republic,[4] in 1805 the Batavian Commonwealth and then in 1806 it changed when Napoleon's brother, Louis Bonaparte, was settled on the throne of the Kingdom of Holland. So it has remained a kingdom. The throne is taken by the next in the family line, male or female, but unlike most monarchs, he or she is allowed to resign and

---

[3] 'Vers l'avenir', *Gazet van Antwerpen* and *Het Belang van Limburg*, July 2009, in a poll of a thousand people.

[4] Named after the Batavi, the German tribe of this area during wars with the Romans.

Queen Juliana of the Netherlands and her family—the bicycling monarchy.
Her daughter, the now Princess Beatrix, an equally keen
cyclist, is second from the right.

does so. After thirty years as queen, Beatrix of Orange abdicated on 30 April 2013 and was succeeded by the sometimes unconventional son, Willem-Alexander, with his queen consort, the Argentine-born Máxima, whom three-quarters of the Netherlands rated at that time as the most popular of the royal family. Will it survive? Yes. There are many bicycles in Holland.

In terms of national opinion, the surest monarchy in continental Europe is Spain's. With interruptions, the monarchy has existed since the Kingdom of Spain was established under Charles I in 1516. There was a republic in 1873–74 and once more in 1931 when King Alfonso XIII went into exile after a national vote favoured a republic. Five years of political changes and republican Popular Front governments led to the formation of a nationalist movement and an attempted military coup that was the start of the Spanish Civil War[5], and that was at first far from successful. It had no credibility when announced in the summer of 1936, but we might remember that Spain was more than a mainland nation. General Emilio Mola's forces were successful in the Canary Islands, Spanish Morocco, Aragon and Seville. The strength lay in the nationalist Army of Africa under General Francisco Franco. By February 1939 Franco was *de facto* leader of Spain and the country would remain a military republic until his death in 1975.

Franco arranged the return to monarchy under King Juan Carlos I. In 2013, it appeared that although there were powerful separatists and republican sympathisers in Spain, some three-quarters of Spaniards would stay with a monarchy and were happy with the notion of Juan Carlos's heir apparent, Felipe, Prince of Asturias. The monarchy is as popular as most others in Europe and costs the Spaniards less than most in Europe: €7.4 million a year at 2010 prices. Will Spain remain a monarchy? Most certainly, and Spain is very Catholic—and although the king is often disliked, the Church of Rome sees the longer-term national stability and unity against separatists as a positive reflection of a conservative combination of Church and Church supporting Spanish monarchy.

We could beware thinking that the percentage polling and politically unthreatening role of the crown protects Europe against constitutional change and that the British, with the world's best-known monarch, is invulnerable to change. If a European monarchy were to declare that it was becoming a republic, the debate over Britain's own constitution would be revived, depending on the circumstances of change elsewhere. While that seems an unthinkable interruption of the British way, events during the first decade or so of the twenty-first century show how a movement might gather pace in the most unlikely circumstances. Europe poses a conundrum that at first sight seems a contradiction. A monarchy dates to absolutism and most certainly predates even an idea that the people would have an overwhelming say in the running of state affairs, from raising taxes to social and collective freedoms, including law-making and the consequences of law-breaking. Therefore the ultimate role of the people to a cause of freedom would be republicanism

[5] 1936–39.

as an expression of total democracy and the distinction of government of the people by the people for the people. That recurring democratic phrasing has its heading as republicanism.

Without republicanism there cannot be, so say the constitutional theorists, total democracy. Whether societies trust total democracy is a different matter and questionable, which is the reason some and seemingly many find monarchy comfortable as a token of individual freedom, confirming a principle of kingship that, in exchange for allegiance, the people will be protected from their natural enemy that is surely government. Yet Europe demonstrates the workings of constitutional anomaly: European monarchies exist in states where the populations are by and large satisfied that they live in democracies. In European monarchies most sovereigns are by their very tolerance a part of the government of the country, albeit a symbolic part. Yet symbolism plays an essential role in politics.

The British psyche sees the political connection with the monarch in an earlier dimension, one that has its origins from more than a thousand years ago: if the king or queen have no political powers, it is true an electorate can take comfort that no Parliament since the mid-seventeenth century has assumed the power to take the dangerous step to remove the monarchy. Therefore, and perhaps illogically, it is a subconscious assumption that there is a constitutional line over which no government will step, unless it would prove politically and economically essential to do so.

Monarchy even without active power does indeed retain its first, even Saxon responsibility: kingship. While the people support the monarchy in principle, no government will get rid of it. The fact that there is no need to at the moment is neither here nor there. However, would the monarchy be weakened at home in the future if one of the fifteen states and crown colonies became republics and divested themselves of the British monarchy? Would the repercussions of republicanism in, say, Antigua bring into question the institution itself? The answer is probably not. Less certain is what may happen if one of the larger territories over which the Queen reigns should break from Great Britain. There are three major candidates for constitutional challenge to the monarchy; two are obvious and one is less so, but much more important. The first two are Australia and Canada.

The British established a global and political empire between the end of Elizabeth I's reign in 1603 and the movement towards independence that, with the exception of the events that led to the United States of America in the eighteenth century, meant the virtual disestablishment of the empire and its responsibilities during the three decades or so after the Second World War. Instead of empire, most of the by-then independent states, most of which were republics, chose to become members of the Commonwealth of former British colonial territories. As republics, the majority within the Commonwealth had presidential heads of state. That left seventeen states with a combined population of some 140 million, including the United Kingdom, with the British sovereign as monarch.[6] One of those states was what became in 1867, by the British North America Act, the self-governing Dominion of Canada. Some of these states have held public votes on the proposition of becoming a republic, including Ghana and South Africa, which both decided in 1960 to become republics; Gambia did so in 1970. Australia held a referendum in 1999 and the proposition to become a republic failed, as did that in Tuvulu in 2008 and Saint Vincent in 2009. The failure to change the relationship with the United Kingdom was partly through political mismanagement. Will Australia become a republic and abandon the monarchy? Yes, it will.

One of the signs that a natural way away from the British crown has long started was a decision by Girl Guides in Australia, who in 2013 rewrote their oath of allegiance and struck out the until then crucial promises for their twenty-eight thousand guiders to serve allegiance to God and the Queen. In an increasingly multi-faith and non-religious Australian society, it was imagined that promises to God would be quietly set aside. Australia's population is largely 'Christian'. Out of the more than sixty per cent of Australians who declared themselves followers of Christianity in the 2011 census, a quarter were Roman Catholics, reflecting the ethnicity of new Australians during post-Second World War migration from Europe, and later, with an influx from

---

[6] Antigua and Barbuda, Australia, The Bahamas, Barbados, Belize, Canada, Grenada, Jamaica, New Zealand, Papua New Guinea, Saint Kitts and Nevis, Saint Lucia, Saint Vincent and the Grenadines, the Solomon Islands, Tuvalu and United Kingdom.

south-eastern Europe, people for whom Christianity was very much steeped in Greek Orthodoxy. A series of 2013 Australian polls suggest that seventy per cent of Australians say that religion has no importance in their daily lives and none in politics.[7] From this it is unremarkable that God was dropped by the Girl Guides. Why drop the reference to the Queen? The Guides believe this a more relevant relationship for Australian girls. Interestingly, this is not the view taken by the Boy Scouts, who for the moment are happy to continue to trust in God and the British monarchy. May this be a sign of a public mood that will be picked up by government? It will not prod government into breaking with the crown. There is every indication, however, that the Australian government will move towards republicanism once the Queen is dead. After next the vote is taken, it is very likely that Australia will have a need not for a governor-general but a president, but it will not be as straightforward as might be imagined.

What of that other long-serving subject of the British monarchy, Canada? In Canada, there is a continuing political debate, particularly within the French-speaking parts, on dropping the monarchy. An important aspect of the public discussion has been the extent to which the monarch is seen as a reflection of the national identity; this is a subject discussed in British terms where that reflection is more easily understood. However, Canadian royalists argue that monarchy maintains the historical identity of Canada and also an aspect rarely given much thought—that monarchy can *make* a nation and its people in a region or even a geographic neighbourhood where difference is sorely tested. There is an argument in Canada that having a monarch emphasises Canada's identity distinctly from the USA. If that may appear unimportant, watch a Canadian's eyes when asked what part of America he or she is from. It is not that monarchy answers the question of confused identity; it is certainly not an imperial scarf tied obviously to the past three centuries of the history of both peoples. Yet it becomes a sub-heading in the very origins of Canada from the seventeenth century and the beginnings of the Hudson's Bay Company.[8]

---

[7] GALLUP WorldView 2009.
[8] In 1670.

These beginnings were followed less than half a century on with the addition of Nova Scotia and Newfoundland into the British imperial and commercial portfolio as spoils from the 1713 Treaty of Utrecht, and, fifty years later, within the Paris Treaty of 1763, Prince Edward Island and Cape Breton Island. In 1840, Lord Durham's supremely clever piece of diplomatic draughtsmanship brought about the union of Upper and Lower Canada, and the first Canadian Parliament the following year. By 1867, and within the British North America Act, Canada had self-government. Yet the federation of Canada was not completed until the twentieth century, when Newfoundland joined in 1949 and modern Canada became complete. It had been a long journey from the eighteenth century, when those, for whatever reasons, crossed from the south during the American War of Independence and became a considerable part of the Georgian protectorate. In modern times, the royal connection is not to be passed over.

A small example of its importance to the monarchy and still presumably to the governments of Canada was illustrated during a brief but significant moment during April 2013, when a not-at-all well Prince Philip flew to Canada to present colours to the 3rd Battalion, The Royal Canadian Regiment, of which he was colonel-in-chief. In Ontario, Prince Philip was twice decorated: with the Companion of the Order of Canada and Commander of the Order of Military Merit by the Governor-General of Canada, David Johnson. Johnson was a Canadian and the twenty-eighth Governor-General since the Confederation. It was a moment that in London raised hardly a media notice beyond publication in the Court Circular. In the Palace and in Canada, it was considered an important occasion.

It would seem inevitable that Canadians question the royal relationship, because it is undoubtedly an imperial hangover, no matter how well meaning and in many quarters it is felt. Yet the connections are often missed in other forms. For example, the Canadian armed forces are closely connected to the United Kingdom military, historically and practically. Canadians are students in British staff colleges, there are many exchange postings and, as is well understood, in past times the Canadians have always been very quick to go to the UK's assistance in times of crisis and war. At one staff-college seminar on loyalty to the crown, Canadians offered the thought that even though their duty was to the government and people of Canada, they could see a case for having Canadian 'royalty' as an apolitical institution. However, Canada, with its increasingly multicultural and multiethnic composition, and a population not particularly touched by recent times past, may have a case for divesting itself of the single obvious connection to its invaded and governed history, even though its independence and wanted role as a dominion dates from the nineteenth century. It would not be difficult to have a president of Canada, but the quasi-independent provinces may set up a debate on the role of provincial premiers. No one is particularly keen to get into the internal and confederate politics of proposing an alternative head of state.

Public opinion in Canada about the monarchy is consistently equally divided during the opening of the twenty-first century. During the 2002 Golden Jubilee celebrations a combined media polling suggested that forty-three per cent of those polled thought it time to break the link to the monarchy, while forty-one per cent thought it should remain. This was not a test of the abolition of the British monarchy. It was a question of keeping the royal association with Canada. The highest rate of abolitionists was in Francophile Quebec, British Columbia and Atlantic Canada. The same polling recorded that males were abolitionists (forty-seven per cent) more than women (thirty-three per cent). Age grouping was not unlike that of polling in the UK. Canadians who wanted to break with the monarchy tended to be middle-aged (forty-five to sixty-four). Royalists were from two identifiable age groups: twenty-five or younger and those of pensionable age, sixty-five and above.[9]

When it came to detailed questioning in that Golden Jubilee Year, sixty-two per cent said that constitutional monarchy defined Canada's identity and on that basis should continue. Equally, sixty-five per cent said that the British royal family should be regarded as celebrities and have no formal governing role in Canada.[10] A similar set of questions by the same polling organisation, Ipsos Reid, showed in April 2005 that of those questioned, fifty-five per cent said that Canada should dissociate

[9] Ekos polling for the Canadian Broadcasting Corporation, Radio-Canada, the *Toronto Star* and *La Presse*, 2002.
[10] Ipsos Reid for *The Globe and Mail* and the Canadian Television Network, 2002.

'from the British Monarchy'. However, this was not revolutionary stuff. All those who wanted a break with royal Britain agreed that dissociation should come not there and then, but at the end of Queen Elizabeth's reign, a similar conclusion to constitutional lawyers and politicians in Australia.

The inference here and from side questions in the polling was clear: the monarch was popular, but the monarchy less so. Moreover, Canadians were uncertain that the line of succession was what they wanted. The idea that some constitutional or historical crossroads should change the mood of tolerance of—presumably not enthusiasm for—monarchy is not surprising in a country with an unbroken line with the British crown. In Canada's case this is historically even less surprising, considering that its people made the conspicuous decision to side with the British monarchy rather than with American patriots and all that followed in the eighteenth century. But what happens when the constitutional change is a highly charged political contradiction within the present order? It is here that we reach the third major constitutional conundrum in a country that for the moment continues to have the Queen at its head of state. That country is Scotland. Could the movement for Scottish independence mean the end of more than four centuries of Anglo-Scottish monarchy?

Future Times

CHAPTER TWELVE

Scotland, the Church of England and the Lords

When James VI of Scotland succeeded to the English monarchy his accession to Elizabeth I's realm created the Union of Crowns and he, without much response from the Cabinet Secretary of his day, Robert Cecil, wished the union to be Great Britain. Cosmetically to support such a grand concept of union, all those born in Scotland after his accession were citizens of England too. During the Protectorate (16 December 1653–25 May 1659) England and Scotland were put together as one state. In 1707 the Act of Union came about partly because the Scots had in 1701 failed to accept the Hanoverian succession. Under the Act of Union, Scotland lost its Parliament, but gained peers and MPs at Westminster, kept its legal system and established Church.

Three centuries on, the movement for separation is more organised than once it was and in 2014 the Scots are due to vote in a referendum on whether to go for independence from the United Kingdom. By summer 2013, it appeared that fewer than a quarter of Scots would vote for independence. What would happen on voting day was quite another matter and throughout 2013 the government in London leaked or suggested details suggesting the Scots would do very badly out of independence. There is no evidence that the London government's warnings

had scared would-be independence supporters in general. Others, especially those who thought they could lose their jobs in a closure of Clyde
yards or elsewhere, were not anyway among the firmest supporters of
independence. What is more, even those doing well out of British EU
membership did not always understand that an independent Scotland
would have to reapply for membership; and with the Scottish economy
as projected for a long time after independence, it was doubtful it would
get in. The general belief was that Britain would veto entry anyway. In
all, it seemed there was a long way to go for those against and for independence if the 2014 referendum would reflect a true desire of Scots.

In the immediate future there is an extra area for discussion that
could touch not only Scots, but the English, Welsh and Northern Irish.
If Scotland became independent, what would the status of the Queen
in Scotland be? Constitutionalists in the London government suggest
privately that the crown would lose Scotland. There is little indication
the Scots have thought this through. Certainly when the debate comes,
as it is bound to in 2014, it will do so against a background that Scots
have become more monarchy-inclined than in a long time.

In 2011, a poll for *Scotland on Sunday* indicated a marked fall in the
republican tendency in Scotland. In 2005, about one-third of Scots
polled wanted to break with the monarchy. In 2011, significantly a
month before the wedding of Prince William to Kate Middleton, only a
quarter identified with that opinion. Just twenty-five per cent thought
that Elizabeth II should be the last British monarch. The leader of the
pro-independence movement, Alex Salmond of the Scottish National
Party, has made it clear that he believes the Queen or her successors
should remain monarch of Scotland if there were to be independence.
The opinion that Prince William should succeed the Queen was up from
twenty-nine to thirty-four per cent, but this is not an issue. Offering
allegiance to the crown, and on present showing the SNP would have
support for this, would mean also that a future monarch would have to
have two coronations—one at Westminster and the other in Scotland.
Charles II was the last monarch to be crowned in both countries.

The important issue that will be debated before the referendum is
that of Scotland's future relationship with the monarchy. For the Queen
or a King Charles to remain effectively head of state, Scotland could

not be a republic and would have to claim constitutional independence within the Commonwealth.

The debate started during the autumn of 2013 with the draft of the White Paper on the structure of a Scottish state. Where the monarch sits in that structure has nothing to do with the crown. She cannot be consulted, because the monarch cannot be expected to express a view, but one constitutional view is very clear in Buckingham Palace. The Queen disapproves enormously of Scottish independence and would see such a change as a weakening not of the authority but the purpose of the crown. If that weakening were to come about, the knock-on effect would not be insignificant, and it would raise important and answerable questions about the purpose of the monarchy not just in Scottish affairs but in other Commonwealth countries where the Queen is head of state and, therefore, issues that until then would not have been bothered with.

(There is a postscript of no constitutional consequence to Scottish independence and the monarchy: the Union Jack would lose its blue background. Some thought it would be needed for the protocols about the royal palaces in Scotland and for acknowledgement of the royal family when it moves into Balmoral for its annual summer holiday.)

Changing relations with Scotland are simple to anticipate because, for the moment at least, the matter hangs on a referendum vote that probably has to reflect a cussedness vote—the opinion of those who might vote yes to rot up the system. It is the unpredictable protest inspired by the occasion. A more searching question must be the future role for the monarch in the Church of England. The future status of the Church will, even during the Queen's reign, be questioned. Should the Church of England remain the state and established Church? If it does not do so, the monarch's authority as the head of a Christian persuasion here on earth is usurped and in that fact a most significant purpose of British monarchy is redundant. Could this at first sight catastrophic event of disestablishment occur? It could and most likely will.

When George III turned aside Pitt the Younger's demand for Catholic emancipation he did so on the unquestionable grounds that by signing such a Bill he (George) would be breaking part of his coronation oath to protect the Church established by Parliament: the Church of England. It was, constitutionally, the correct decision and apart from reminding us that George III is a far too much maligned king it demonstrated the authority and responsibility of the sovereign as governor of the Church. Henry VIII had established through Parliament that the state owned the Church. His reasoning was beyond his needs for Anne Boleyn, whatever some Catholic lobbies would think. Certainly he demanded that the pope should not interfere with England's 'empire'—that is, homeland. The time of Henry was the time of necessary reformation in Europe and the Church in Britain was part of that reform, although not beholden to its values. So what came to be known as the Anglican Communion had its origins in the British Reformation and was by means of its legislative creation part of the establishment and the ordinances of a slowly developing political elite. Nothing has changed. That is why we should ask: if the Church of England were 'floated', that is disestablished, would the monarchy have lost one of its three reasons to exist—the other two being the monarchy as the final authority for government legislation to be enacted and national identity? These three issues—the Church of England, the signatory of legislation, the connection with the people— are the essential ones that set the monarchy aside from an alternative head of state. For example, the British monarch is apparently apolitical; not all heads of state are. An American president, for example, does not have an established church, because in spite of the open religiosity of American society there is no church governed by the laws of Congress and because of his or her short reign a president cannot be said to reflect the identity of the nation.

In the less easily definable level of a monarch reflecting a nation's identity, it is more likely that the population, even when showing affection for the crown, is today so multicultural and financially varied that this once easy definition has lost its features and even purpose. British society has few feelings for any institution and it could be that once the disestablishment debate among the small Anglican church-going population (about eleven per cent of the national population and declining) was done and the hands wrung, the British would do little more than get on with the new ways they have created since the end of the 1970s. Part of the debate would be the position of the monarch, but a nation that polls against an institution with a royal cypher will not necessarily be against the monarchy.

In polls that respond to questions about the monarch, the royal family and the institution it heads, there are few distractions. A person polled may be a monarchist, or a republican, or just a regular person who gets along with the subject of monarchy until asked to consider what he or she thinks. There is, unless the respondent is a committed republican, no alternative on offer. Questions about the Church and its establishment are far more complex and less likely to encourage gut answers as the one on monarchy. The reasons for this are all laid out in the cast of society during the past half-century. Pertinent to questions about the established Church is the small percentage of the population who are members of the Church of England, against the mix of other Christian persuasions and variations in other religions, such as Judaism, Islam, Humanism and so on. There is one apparent distinction between two of the main Christian denominations in the United Kingdom: members of the established Church of England are likely to approve of the monarch. Roman Catholics are less likely to approve. But what would be the mood of the Anglican Church leaders?

A recent Archbishop of Canterbury, Doctor Rowan Williams, who grew up as a member of the disestablished Church of Wales and was once its archbishop, never spoke against disestablishment. In fact, he understood the integrity of Synod being able to vote on its own counsel without having a Westminster political synod having a final say on the Church's business. Since 1919, Synod (formerly the Church Assembly) has voted on Church Measures and then has had to send them to both Houses of Parliament. Parliament cannot amend those Measures, but votes to accept or reject. Its decision is final. In Church domestic affairs and arrangements, Synod can debate and then pass Canons— its own laws. But they have to be approved by the monarch and the sovereign has to sign Canons into law. The sovereign is not allowed an active opinion on these Canons of the crown's Church. He or she has to accept the guidance of the Home Secretary of the day. This is yet another example of the entirely ceremonial role of the sovereign, who always has to be an Anglican and to protect the Church as ordered in the Coronation Oath, although in reality there is nothing the Queen or a future King Charles could do to stop changes approved by Parliament.

The Anglican laity, usually reflecting a conservative and Conservative mindset, is to remain established. Without much opposition, the Anglicans sense that society is wobbly on almost everything institutional at the moment. Banking, law, health care, investment and Parliament are openly mistrusted or worse. To analyse the future of the establishment of the state Church would add to that public despair of all these once trusted matrices of British society.

What the public may feel about a Church in which few of them worship is difficult to test. In 2011 a British election poll, using a close-on nineteen thousand sample, asked if the Church of England should keep its status as the official established Church of England. More than half said that it should, twenty-two per cent did not mind either way and sixteen per cent wanted disestablishment. Unsurprisingly, older people wanted to keep everything as it is and the eighteen-to-twenty-four age group wanted change. The political response was also unsurprising. Sixty-nine per cent of Tories were to keep an established Church of England. Just under half of Labour and Lib Dems polled wanted change. In other polls, among declared Christians there was some indication of the laity view of the monarch's role. An average of a third, mainly the over-sixty-fives, thought the monarch should continue as head of the Anglican Church and more than half opposed the position.

The image of the monarchy within this questioning is supported elsewhere during this period, in around 2012. For example, eighty-five per cent of professed Christians were proud of Queen Elizabeth II and her role as governor of the Church. Pride in the monarchy among these churchgoers was less certain when other members of the royal family were addressed. Forty-one per cent were proud of Prince Charles. There is a single view among some clergy and some laity that if the state Church is to be disestablished from Parliament, that would come during a reign of Charles who, it is imagined, would be open to a wider view than previous monarchs. It is a difficult contemplation. A monarch is crowned into the Church of England. Unlike its parishioners, a sovereign cannot lapse from his or her responsibilities.

The further question on modern concepts of disestablishment is: is it just a routine to debunk and deflower every institution? The Anglican Church has long become something that is good to have and it has mostly inoffensive buildings. Its relevancy to most lives is the fact that it is there, and by and large even non-communicants know what it does. Contrary to myth, the devil does not have the best tunes; the Church of England does, if rarely sung by many. Yet it does have a constitutional relevance. Any established Church is governed by the link to a political forum. Because the Church of England has an official status through Parliament and, for historical reasons, as a representative of the people, guardian of parliamentary and political values, and low representative of the monarch, it nominates twenty-six bishops into the House of Lords. The Church therefore has a political role and a political vote in the nation's revising chamber. An evangelical would think the Church was better out than in.

Will disestablishment take place? On evidence of the changing role of institutions, there is no reason why it ever should. However, with declining relevance in British society the more evangelical Anglican wing is very likely to see the disestablishment debate as an apparent opportunity for, to put it crudely, what would be a Church of England makeover that would be enhanced by being in closer communion with not the Catholic Church but with the non-conformists. Disestablishment will be, on anecdotal evidence at least, the saving of an institution in which many of its adherents sense they are in the same position as those who petitioned King James in 1603. When that debate is final, it will ironically be because Parliament says so. The monarch will have no say, but will, as a further irony, have to sign the Bill into law. Would there be an echo of George III in a future King Charles?

There is a further consideration in connection with monarchy, Church and Parliament: Lords reform. Successive governments since the 1960s have pledged Lords reform. However, no government has followed through on these ambitions as far as a workable draft proposal that could get wide debate.

Will the House of Lords be reformed? Yes. Nothing can be properly contemplated until the matter of Scottish independence is resolved—for the moment at least. The constitutional ructions would make reform an impossible task for years after a yes-to-independence vote. It is impossible to ask the governing powers of a new Lords without first setting out who will be governed. We have also to understand that whichever way the 2014 vote falls, the British constitution (unwritten, as it is unimportant) will undergo changes. These changes could, in not too much of a long run, lead to the United Kingdom becoming a federation. A federation of four nations would mean radical reform of both Houses of Parliament, with little possibility of the hereditary system surviving in a totally elected upper chamber (whatever its function), including such roles as the Lord Great Chamberlain linking Westminster to the monarchy. It is difficult to see that the sovereign would have even the present contrived authority in his or her own kingdom. When will this reform come to something? If Scotland broke away, reform would have to start within the transition. If the vote were close, reform would be a natural response. Even if the answer were no, the option of doing nothing would have gone. Thus Lords reform will happen in the lives of the now middle-aged. Constitutionally, the monarch's role will be diminished. The voting figures seen earlier suggest that there would be majority indifference to that loss of symbolism.

CHAPTER THIRTEEN

In Conclusion—Or Not?

T he primary purpose of the royal family is to breed healthy and long-lived future kings and queens from first-in-line stock. Having done so, the royal family can then settle into the role of global celebrity and ignore the thought that it has no other function than to please the majority of people by its very presence. The British public is content with this arrangement. There is no need to change the principle, only the way it is managed.

While institutional reform is a constant in British public life, the debate is always about reform. The monarchy is the only institution that gets questioned on its very existence. Banks, Church, Parliament and law are scrutinised, but no one asks whether we need them. There is the very vulnerability of the argument for monarchy. Every British institution but monarchy is needed to run, regulate and bring together the several aspects of society. Monarchy does not do this, however popular it is. If the monarchy went, British society would not. A generation and the second election of a president is probably all it would take for a new order to be accepted. Although the monarchy has no part to play in the national economic performance, influenced as it is by global affairs, a bad economy with a president would encourage a longing for times past; a good economy under a new system would beat nostalgia on points.

All the above settles down to the last questions: will the British monarchy survive until the time of an accession of Prince George of Cambridge and if it does what will it look like? The first part of a complex answer lies in the imagery of the monarchy, but most of all in the perception the people have of their Queen.

Elizabeth came to the throne with all the appearance of a vulnerable princess in some constitutional fairytale from Britain's imperial past. She sold more television sets during one week than anyone had or ever would. Strapped for cash, a government that truly feared a newly powerful Germany and Stalin's gathering Soviet bloc in Eastern Europe had raided every Whitehall purse for rebuilding the Royal Navy, the Army and the RAF. So come the autumn of 1952, when the Queen was finally persuaded to allow the coronation the following June to be televised, not even the foundations for the array of planned television masts were dug. North-east miners threatened to march because they had no television service for the coronation. Hurriedly, work started on moorland transmitters and crews were sent in vans to retransmit signals through wire and string equipment. Reception was poor and in some places nonexistent, but come the day the people began tuning the 2.7 million television sets in the kingdom. More than twenty million gathered round them to watch. 'Vivat Regina' echoed through stalls and pews and around arches of Westminster Abbey, and then across the globe. It remains the most repeated image of, and set the pattern of references to regal composure that is the Queen's badge of office. Whatever followed, the polling numbers always saw the Queen as above the controversies of royalty, monarchy and the royal family.

Even the supposedly blazing row with Philip during the 1954 tour of Australia—the Queen apparently hurled tennis racket and sports shoes after the retreating figure of her husband—failed to disturb the image, thanks to an Australian film crew which still went along with the then protocol that nothing should be shot, never mind shown to embarrass the Queen. But that was the period of absolute image control. It meant that, for example, the Palace worked on the principle that only that which appeared in the London Gazette was to be reported by the media, an institution that the Queen's first press secretary, Commander Richard Colville, thought full of at least scallywags; it was as if Colville worked on the notion that what the monarch did was no one's business.

To support this view, he had the power to tell newspaper editors what they could and could not report; this was the 1950s and so editors tended to accept this line. The step-change came in 1968 when Colville retired and an Australian, William Heseltine, replaced him. The era of Prince Charles's 'crowning' as Prince of Wales set the way for the younger royals to become part of the public family; the filming of Richard Cawston's *Royal Family* remains almost half a century later the single moment when the Palace opened up. It did not remain open at that level again, although a later film about life aboard the royal yacht *Britannia* came close. Undoubtedly, *Royal Family* got too close to the subject. It was an intimate portrayal in very good taste. Yet it had a drawback: the monarchy suffered once some of the mystique had been set aside.

The public wanted to know more about the royal family in the late 1960s. It was an era of revelation anyway. If that same public believed it knew what was going on in that most prestigious of circles, more was to come with the television interviews of Prince Charles talking about his adultery and Princess Diana talking about hers. If the public thought it knew everything about the private lives of Charles and Diana, it was finding out that it had only the gossip. What was not remarked upon was the fact there was nothing new in royal bedroom tales. The patronymic 'Fitz' for a royal bastard son has an honourable and considerably common heritage.

The Hanoverian dynasty from one century into another was full of lurid accounts of royals bed-hopping and out-of-wedlock loyalties. The passions, even romances, of Victoria's son, the then Prince of Wales and later Edward VII, were common gossip and even common knowledge. What was odd about the Charles and Diana exploits was that in the most permissive age of the later part of the twentieth century, the British expressed surprise and lined up to pass judgement. Adultery has been on many a royal *curriculum vitae*, but here were the supposedly liberated British, with one of the biggest rates of unfaithfulness, if not the biggest, in Europe, expressing the rights and wrongs of the situation. Behind this mood was and has partly been the anomaly of the stability exhibited by the Queen, wherein protocol formal and behaviour informal are carefully set and executed, and at the same time the public sees Elizabeth II as head of one of the more dysfunctional royal families in the nation's history.

Of the Queen's four children, only one is still in the original marriage. Her elder sons, Prince Charles and Prince Andrew, were often the subjects of media stories that certainly did not always reflect the worthier sides of their personalities and lives. The media debate about what royalty should have done when Diana, Princess of Wales, died did not have much real substance and seemed anyway to have glided past the figure of the Queen. Whatever the criticism, when she and Prince Philip eventually returned to London and stepped from the Palace to inspect the carpet of flowers for Diana, there was quiet respect and concern as there might have been for any other grieving family, even if the public had little to go on in making any judgement that anyone but the young princes were in grief.

The 'image thing'—as President George W. Bush used to call official PR projects—is now everything for the Palace. There are fewer than twenty people in the three royal family press offices (Buckingham Palace, Saint James's Palace and Clarence House) handling the most bankable brand in the world. Their purpose is to keep the image on the straight and narrow, that is, to make certain that the media worldwide understands that nothing in British royalty is sensational and that what is seen as sensational is all very ordinary. It is a unique brand that does not compete, does not have a market share and since the first half of the seventeenth century does not worry about takeovers. Into this is melted the continuous reassurances for royalty offered by opinion pollsters, especially the most experienced of them all, GALLUP.

Polling groups appear to ask the hard questions, but rarely do because the standard ones have predictable answers and always include the questions that matters above all. Does a country need this or that monarchy anymore? Why should the people pay for crowned heads who do nothing else but open hospitals and sign Acts that do not need signing once government has decided it is going to enact them into law anyway? No other major institution is questioned about its very existence. No other head of that institution has to justify its existence as much as a monarch does. This is the case across Europe. In other places of course—Saudi Arabia, Thailand, the sultanates of the Gulf—it is a treasonable act even to question the existence, never mind the role, of the monarch or sultan.

In Europe, republicanism is no longer seen as a revolutionary movement. To question the idea of monarchy is part of a protest at the very strident end of political and constitutional argument. No longer do republicans plot actively to tear down the gates and crumble the walls of monarchy. Republicanism, perhaps because it has rarely in recent years figured in large percentages of populations, has not been an active threat. It is rather a political, social and philosophical reflection, and it takes place in a democracy that contains the object of discontent. Republicans commit no act of treason within European democracies, because they campaign against an aspect of that democracy, the choice of the people to retain a monarchy.

When the pollsters have reported, republicanism has figured nowhere particularly in recent times, when younger people questioned have found new interests in monarchy by the coming together of Kate Middleton and Prince William, and more recently the birth of Prince George. It is almost as if William and Kate are not seen as real royalty, but just nice guys. The average person questioned cannot begin to know that beneath those smiles and schoolgate waves are people who have to honour protocols and behaviours totally alien to those who would see them as their peers. It is important to understand this relevant ignorance to judge the importance of respondents to questions on perceptions of royalty.

A younger age group may be certain that they can identify with the Cambridges as fellow youngsters, as sons and daughters, and even as fellow married couples and young parents. But once the throne is claimed and the crown worn, the people's prince and princess are far less likely to be identifiable. Notwithstanding the close-knit community of the royal family, the monarch must be bowed, bobbed and curtsied to by children and closer. No one is exempt from acknowledging the authority of the monarch. Even Prince Philip standing alongside his wife must show his allegiance and sing the National Anthem loudly.

Once monarch, no one, however close they think they may be, is allowed to cross the line that is intimacy. The kind of casual remark made to a friend cannot be made to the monarch. That assumes too much intimacy. A simple blank stare is enough to remind a confidant that an invisible line has been crossed. The commoner can understand that he or she has assumed too much. The monarch has to live within her or his own rules. None must be close enough for familiarity to risk the authority of the monarch. Thus the monarch's life beyond the inner royal family is a simple protocol: none may cross the line. A sovereign may never be on first-name terms with a commoner, for the commoner may never be on first-name terms with a sovereign. It is thus best to avoid one-sided familiarity.

This single distinction is a reminder that few doubt that the ruler is the most privileged person in the realm, yet the monarch reflects the identity of the people over which she or he rules, including the least privileged. This has nothing to do with when to curtsy or when men should give a neck bob. There is a sense that hereditary monarchy is god-like. Yet it sits not on a cloud, leaving others to protect its existence. The British monarchy is a working institution that has the advantage of having had its leader for more than sixty years, and therefore, through the thick and thin of her reign, the institution has survived. The people, almost without exception, approve. There could be little questioning of the general satisfaction of living within the British monarchy of Elizabeth II. It has been a harmless reign that has inspired affection for the Queen, although disaffection with the wider royal family has increased. Without this sovereign, it could well be that the British monarchy has run its course, while fulfilling its first duty: to continue the line.

How that public would feel if misfortune presented a Queen Eugenie or Beatrice (currently sixth- and seventh-in-line) is for speculation. From this we can see the danger that a nation happy with a monarch may change its mind if the next-in-line is disappointing. Fortunately for the system, there is always the follow-on heir. That is why in the unlikely event that King Charles proves unpopular, there is no doubt that on present opinion poll showing a King William would have the opportunity to restore the nation's joy at being subjects of a constitutional monarchy.

A week after the July 2013 birth of Prince George of Cambridge (students of the English Civil War might have hoped for a Royalist Oxford rather than a Cromwellian Cambridge connection), Britain's most popular royalist newspaper, the *Sunday Telegraph*, splashed the headline: 'The Royal family can reign over us for ever—Poll shows confidence at an all-time high—Republicans lose out to Prince George'.

The source of this celebration was a survey for the newspaper suggesting that seventy-four per cent were confident that Prince George would one day be king.[1] Nine per cent surveyed thought the first born of the Duke and Duchess of Cambridge would not be king, because by the likely time of succession (half a century on) Britain would have become a republic. Two years earlier, in 2011, most opinion polls suggested that twenty-five per cent believed Britain would become a republic within that period. The popularity of the leading members of the British royal family has not much shifted during the past three or four decades, so the figures were not surprising, especially after a globally covered royal birth the previous week.

The most popular group, headed by the Queen, consisted of the Cambridges and Prince Harry. Apart from the sovereign, the leading royal personality in the polling was the Duchess of Cambridge, especially among the eighteen-to twenty-four age group, and importantly more women than men voted for the Cambridges. Prince Harry's more macho image, collected in Afghanistan and Las Vegas, had him rated third most popular royal. In league terms out of a hundred and in answer to the question about which member of the royal family was most admired, the Queen got twenty per cent of the vote, William nineteen per cent, Harry seventeen per cent, Kate twelve per cent, the Duke of Edinburgh and the Prince of Wales four per cent, the Princess Royal three per cent and the Duchess of Cornwall one per cent.

Public opinion of the royals had not much shifted, but produced a difference in the succession. Forty-two per cent supported the Prince of Wales's right to the throne and thirty-eight per cent voted for the generation skip. The figures were predictable, but contained two telling results. Fifty-seven per cent of those polled were not convinced that the royal family was worth the £36.1 million taxpayer-funded Sovereign Grant. About half the country did not feel the royal family was giving value for money. The second figure is not so damning, but suggests that not all is as it would sometimes seem in royalist camps. Another question was: if Britain did not have the royal family, would the nation be worse or better off? More than half thought the UK would be worse off without royalty, but forty-seven per cent were not at all sure about that.

---

[1] ComRes survey published in the *Sunday Telegraph*, 28 July 2013.

Equally, the republicans have always been and always will be a small minority in the polling tables. The ComRes figures endorsed this and made the point that even republicans do not think there will be a going of royalty during the century. Certainly the mood reflected the idea that there is no need to change the system and never has been—even the Roundheads came to understand that. Moreover, the question of whether it is morally right to have a monarchy has never much come to anything in the British Isles. There has never been a convincing moral argument for replacement. There might be an instinct to wonder how it is, in an age of realism and justification, a nation the size of the United Kingdom and with the social complexities of that society can continue to support such a privileged group as monarchy. Curiously, supporters are not entirely buoyed by the polling evidence. They resort to questionable claims such as royalty being good for tourism (are there no tourists in France or Italy?), rather than pointing to the overwhelming support of the public and the facts that Britain has had a monarchy for a thousand years and the majority still like it that way; and what would the public miss if the monarchy went?

The first thing missing would be imagery. Only a monarch can dress so ostentatiously. Plumes, sashes, stars of honours, unwon medals and multiple crowns all on one figure at the same time would look pantomimic on any other individual. White-hosed and buckled-shoe page bearers scarlet to the waist, Gentlemen at Arms, Silver and White Sticks in Waiting, Cap Bearers, Lords Great Chamberlain, and breached and silk-gowned courtiers all walking backwards, bowing but none expecting a smile in return, could only be in imperial attendance. Golden coaches, stiff-armed waves to cheering streets, and clip-clopping and jingling horses with breast-plated heroes astride them could only be a regal procession with bands in clarion path. No president, whatever his or her honours, would be so gilded and attended. No president could ever be borne in open landau or state gold, with Blues and Royals in escort.

Second, there are duties. No president would be there to open three hundred personal letters a day and fifty day centres a year, to lunch and dine deserving folk and never, almost never, be known to have said anything at any of these events. And no president would be able to move so slowly. Royalty never moves quickly. It makes a steady progress through lines of posy children; a half-turn with a surprised look at kerbside flag wavers; a soft but distinct inquiry—'Have you come far?'—with no heard answer to what is said. No president could ever say nothing memorable. A monarch can say nothing to fill a postcard in sixty and more years. But a monarch is memorable for all that, because a monarch can be cheered and even adored from a distance.

Third, a nation would miss the symbol of its own identity. There is some anecdotal evidence that of course not all but the majority of the world knows who Queen Elizabeth II is. The monarchy is a curious 'Made in Britain' emblem and is not always respected, but it exists and remains a constant in an individual's identity, particularly as national identity is almost exclusively about how others see us.

Fourth, the British would miss effortless continuity. The longevity of royalty and its barely changing pageantry and imagery are sturdy and lasting reassurances that society is not a now institution; they reassure in an apolitical sense that a core trait in national character is, while socially divisive, sometimes for a common purpose. A president, depending on the voting system, can arrive with half the nation against him or her. A president would know inside eight years that it was time to go and his or her supporters would know that much earlier. A monarch is for life.

It would seem from these three easily challenged conceptions that there would be no point in the British abandoning a constitutional monarchy. We return to the fact that monarchy is the only institution about which we ask: why have it any more? Toxic institutions that touch daily lives are only asked to repair themselves. Monarchists praise the House of Windsor for modernisations during the past thirty or so years, certainly since the image blips at the death of Diana. But has there really been much change? The Palace media setup runs what the late press secretary, Commander Colville, would have called a very tight ship.

The Diamond Jubilee year confirmed the Queen's popularity and the rest took care of itself. British royalty media coverage, while not necessarily obsequious, has little chance but to follow directions from the Palace press office and to some extent their own news desks. The days of royal revelation are gone, for the moment, and news organisations plan for the inevitable. The first, the birth of a new heir, has come with the

Palace and Prince George in command of coverage. The second, concern over the continuing, not always good health of Prince Philip, is all in hand with media planning desks. The course of royal breeding for the future and the role of the heirs apparent appear in hand. This leaves the question of what next, rather than speculation about survival.

Again, from everything we have explored, from instincts, history, precedent, institutional reform, opinion polling, and political and public mood, the future of the British monarchy is assured in the shorter term, but in spite of the wishes in the 2013 polling, not in the longer term.

The transition from the reign of Elizabeth to Charles has started. In 2013 there were two illustrations of old order shifting slightly— not its authority, but its duties. The first was at the State Opening of Parliament in May 2013, at which Prince Charles sat side-throned, while the enthroned Queen read her 'My Government Will' speech. With the Prince of Wales was his wife wearing Queen Mary's Boucheron tiara, loaned by the Queen. That is not a fashion note. Its significance should not be ignored; nor should the brooch and sash of the Royal Victorian Order, the Monarch's personal, gifted order. It is not so long since the Queen refused to have Camilla's name spoken. They now greet with kisses.

The second illustration has much to do with a recognition that the Queen is in her late eighties, and Prince Philip in his nineties and not at his past best. The Queen decided that she did not wish to go far from Prince Philip, nor did she want the exertion of a long-haul flight; so it was decided that Prince Charles, with his wife, would represent the Queen at the November 2013 Commonwealth Heads of Government meeting in Sri Lanka. These meetings take place every four years. It is reasonable to believe that barring accidents Prince Charles will be at the next meeting too. The increasingly sovereign role for Prince Charles means that some of his duties will be shifted to Prince William, some to Prince Harry and maybe even more to the Duke of York.

With the anticipation that Prince William will take on many of the royal duties of first heir, he may have to end his military career. With an increased royal duties list he would become a passenger in the Royal Air Force or, should he choose to return to his original service, the Army. That decision would be taken by the autumn of 2013 if, for no other reason, everyone in the RAF and at the Palace would need to know what he was doing for the following two or three years. Both Palace and RAF plan that far ahead. Out of the RAF, William would be more visible in public duties and that would increase the speculation on the succession: Charles or William? There is no question that Charles will, if health holds, be the next monarch. The question comes of when. Could the Queen decide that age plays tricks with stamina and that she does not wish to be a remote figure just to make guest appearances as monarch, and that she might even want to retire into Queen Motherdom? There is nothing but a sense of duty that would prevent the Queen following Queen Beatrix of the Netherlands and King Albert of the Belgians in 2013, and abdicating in favour of a son. The mechanism and paperwork are already in place.

Clearly the precedent is the going of Edward VIII in December 1936. Two points should be noted: Edward had to sign a declaration that he would go; and, importantly, the constitutional authority of the abdication document insisted that none of his descendants would be able to claim the throne. The crown passed to Edward's brother, who was a descendant of George V and not of Edward VIII.

The legislation that the then Prime Minister, Stanley Baldwin, laid before the Commons and that sent Edward from the throne was *His Majesty's Declaration of Abdication Act 1936*:

An Act to give effect to His Majesty's declaration of abdication; and for purposes connected therewith [11 December 1936]. Whereas His Majesty by His Royal Message of the tenth day of December in this present year has been pleased to declare that He is irrevocably determined to renounce the Throne for Himself and His descendants, and has for that purpose executed the Instrument of Abdication set out in the Schedule to this Act, and has signified His desire that effect thereto should be given immediately:

And whereas, following upon the communication to His Dominions of His Majesty's said declaration and desire, the Dominion of Canada pursuant to the provisions of section four of the M1 Statute of Westminster 1931 has requested and consented to the enactment of this Act, and the Commonwealth of Australia,

the Dominion of New Zealand, and the Union of South Africa
have assented thereto...

The obvious differences would be the circumstances of the Queen's
abdication. There is no unpleasantness to overcome and there is no
question of the Queen's descendants not inheriting. But the Edward VIII
abdication document is a reminder that other countries over which he
was monarch had to approve the Act. An irregular change of monarchy
may not have the same circumstances in modern times, but the approval
of fifteen other states that have the Queen as head of state would have
to be consulted. The same situation has arisen from the current legislation to change the order of accession; the British Parliament has
voted that the first born, boy or girl, can became heir to the throne.
The fifteen other legislatures have to ratify that process. Not all have.
It could even be in radical times in some Commonwealth and colonial
political systems that the British legislation could be used as a reason to
force an issue and consideration of whether to retain the Queen as head
of state. Any abdication, however understandable, could be used as a
similar excuse. This is not yet an issue, but it is not one that the Palace
and government have ignored. On the assumption that abdication is
unlikely, what would be the next event in the process of maintaining
monarchy?

At the death of the Queen, Charles, assuming he survives his mother,
will be crowned king with Camilla his wife entitled Princess Consort.
The new monarch could insist that she become Queen Camilla. For the
moment, it is not an important issue. With good health and cheerful-
ness, the monarchy would continue until William is crowned and then,
perhaps by the 2060s or 2070s, a George will return to the British
throne. Or is that too simple, considering the earlier discussions? Yes,
it is too simple.

The monarchy's style will change. Prince Charles, although a stickler
for formality and a demander of respect for royal positions and persons,
is not inclined to abandon ideas, and will, without too many references to carbuncles, make his views known to people he believes can
act on them. Will that change anything? The Queen is easy to vote for
in opinion polls. Most are unaware of any of her opinions and so she
draws few criticisms when it comes to MORI time. The image is voted

The Royal Family, the size of which is decided by the monarch.
A new sovereign will inevitably reduce the size of the balcony scenes.

on. Charles will know that he will be voted on for his opinions as well as his dignity as king. It will take time for his popularity to rise. A consequence could so easily be people taking sides on his monarchy. That does not happen with the Queen. National debates will not involve the king, but his opinion could become relevant and therefore his could be a Georgian monarchy, although not quite in the manner of George III, of whom Charles, versus Pitt, is a champion.

The biggest change will be slower to spot. There is much talk of the oft-cited hangers-on in the royal family. Much of the funding for them comes through the Queen's income from the Duchy of Lancaster; they are not directly a drain on the public purse as suggested. Moreover, the 'lesser' royals do a lot of work as patrons of and visitors to projects and organisations that would otherwise have no highlights and maybe too few fund-raising boosts through royalty. Nationally, the Duke of York is not over-popular because of his reputation as 'Air Miles Andy', as he is dubbed by the media, yet there is a diary full of visits that make all the difference to the organisations concerned. The Duke and Duchess of Gloucester have a visiting workload that amounts to a full-time job. Yet there is a case for slimming this side of the royal firm down. It is not a matter of royalty taking less part in the informal as well as the formal ways of the realm.

Society is changing its priorities even to the point of judging the impacts of lesser royals and the cost-weigh against the effort of having them open, speak and handshake an event. The new monarch, the Cambridges and Prince Harry will do more, while the others will not have these roles. Royalty's role will be less visible. It will not see an immediate change of pace, but it is a thought that in, say, just twenty years from now, the young in Britain will be relating to Prince George of Cambridge instead of as they do now with the Duke and Duchess of Cambridge. His middle-aged parents will, all things being equal, be preparing for the accession.

Within that time two institutions discussed earlier will have changed or will be heading towards change. The House of Lords will be reformed down to an elected chamber. That will not mean the end of the aristocracy of inherited peerages, but it will mean the end of the right to govern. The medieval heritage will have played its part, but will do no more. With the passing of an unelected element in the Lords, the role of the aristocracy and the line to the throne will be diminished. The monarch's role will not be weakened, because it has no strength anyway. It will still be the monarch's government, but the already ceremonial role will have less meaning.

The Church of England will begin a transition towards the most important piece of legislation in its history since the sixteenth-century Act of Supremacy. It will, probably for its own good, become disestablished. The role of the monarch in that Church will not exist other than by patronage.

There is yet another change in the way British society holds together that will touch the institution of monarchy, because the whole British way will be changing. We should take note of the events in public squares during 2011, 2012 and 2013, and anticipate that this is the start rather than a passing phase of radicalisation and even rebellion. The global rebellion has two things in common: first, a sense that young, well-educated men and women do not have the opportunities that their intellectual energies and ambitions expected; second, a sense in every continent that government does not listen or in some cases does not care.

In the United Kingdom's case, the warnings came a decade before the Tahrir Squares of the world lit up. The protest was in the march against going to war in Iraq. The marchers made no difference. They were heard, but not listened to. Government, maybe rightly at the time, believed it knew better. But that march signalled the frustrations of people believing they were no longer listened to and perhaps never had been. After all, the Jarrow marchers achieved no more and they were starving. As an overview, we are seeing society after society expressing frustration and dissatisfaction. Those who would say that those demonstrations took place in places that would not have the same opportunities of expressing themselves that British society has should mark well the power of social media, of a growing electorate which, without knowing what it was doing, voted out the main political parties in Britain so that a coalition had to be formed.

We have seen global change that will not stop in the Middle East. Brazil has proved that. This is not world revolution, but the sense of change is not to be ignored and it is visited in Europe with unrelenting unrest in Bulgaria—a European Union member.

The lesson of all unrest, from the eighteenth-century French

Revolution onwards, is that impeccably managed constitutional institutions are not invulnerable to change. The means of communication
among the dissatisfied are growing at an almost unpredictable rate. At
the time of writing, Google was unheard of a decade ago by the majority
in Tahrir Square. Today 'Google' is a verb. The capability of events and
unstructured leadership to change opinion, rouse dormant thoughts
and bring them to an unpredictable radical state, at a time when other
changes, such as the above-mentioned, are mooted, will affect the
way even British society thinks about its traditional structure. There
is another part to this thought: either British royalty is the constant
necessary to avoid radicalisation, or it will perhaps be a target for that
new way.

Opinion pollsters ask all the time what the public thinks of the
monarch, the princes and princesses, and the monarchy itself. It asks
whether we want to keep the monarchy, as if it were only a moral or
constitutionally philosophical question. It is not. There is hardly
any way that the public could rise up against the British monarchy.
It is unthinkable that there could be circumstances that would bring
hundreds of thousands onto British streets in protest of a system that
over ten centuries has served the nation better than most institutions.
In modern times monarchies are rarely challenged as institutions.
Certainly in the case of the British monarchy, the sovereign now has
only ceremonial powers and is simply an international celebrity with a
not always dignified house. Few would be bothered to join any organised protest against the House of Windsor. Only the small numbers of
republicans in British society would blame the royal family and that
thousand-year-old system for the greater ills of a nation. The stated
aim of members of the protest group *Republic* is that they 'simply want
what's best for Britain'. Given that most public polling suggests that
people only want what's best for themselves and because royalty does
not, by and large, disturb that self-interest, then the institution is safe
for the moment.

It is therefore changes to institutions and indifference that could
damage the means and ways of monarchy in the United Kingdom. There
will always be a day centre to open but would there be a place in a future
British senate—and surely there will be one—for a sovereign to declare
My Government will, when clearly government will no longer be the

sovereign's even by today's degree of token authority? A disestablished church in which fewer than ten per cent of the population worships will not be one that will have a need for a supreme governor with no powers at all to defend its authority nor to protect it from the assumed emancipation of more organised religions as once did George III. With that single task removed from the Coronation Oath, as it will be, then the monarch's only authority is in his or her personal devotion to the institution.

Furthermore, it has to be contemplated that republicanism's next success will not be in the UK but in some countries outside the British Isles that retain the monarch as head of state. When the Queen dies, both Australia and Canada will be the first to rethink their need for a British monarch as head of state. Within a decade or two, the British sovereign will rule no more territory than did the Stuarts. A King Charles perhaps, a King William almost certainly, will not have to make world tours to loyal subjects.

There is then, a sense that the monarchy is moving to being something only grand and impressive in its own home and then not as before and therefore with hardly any role.

Moreover, the future is not about protest but changing order in the world. A future British government will have the responsibility of recognising that it is economically and politically convenient for Britain to be a republic with a voted-for president—certainly within fifty years. This is not because the people wish to get rid of royalty. Instead there is already a gradual shift in political emphasis in the United Kingdom, with all the outside influences only now imagined that could make it inevitable that the nations would be better protected from political and economic disaster with an elected president, an unelected Cabinet, and an elected senate and lower house.

Here is the first irony: the opinion polls will not deliver the black-cap verdict on British monarchy. A not-too-distant political and economic future will do that. The order of economic viability for Britain could so easily create a need for a totally different form of government: a hundred-seat senate, a five hundred-seat house of representatives, an unelected cabinet of executive power and therefore, a president. The second irony is that the American system developed from European-inspired ideological thought will work better in Europe and in particular in the United Kingdom. There is little to suppose that change will not come about; it will not be for ideological reasons but because there is a political and economic sense line running through the United Kingdom's imagined place in global positioning. Moreover the illusion of the popularity of the monarchy is contained in the premise with which we started: the monarchy that was founded in the promise of kingship is today maintained on the foundation created by the sitting sovereign. When Queen Elizabeth II dies the British and Commonwealth feeling about the monarchy—not just the living monarch—will be tested. We must forget present opinion about the future kings. Prince Charles will be an old man before he gets the throne. Prince William and even Prince George will be middle-aged. Public delight and devotion will not be based on present feelings towards the next and the younger generations.

Furthermore, we live in ages in which technology has shown how lifestyles, opinions and ways of living and behaviour to the great institutions can change in a single generation. We have seen that throughout this book as we shifted from times past, present and what next in time. Between now (2013) and the projected period of the suggested accession of a King George, British values will have changed at a greater pace than at any time in the past 1000 years.

Political and economic reality, together with instant options provided by technology and up to now hard to imagine social reasoning, will see radical changes in society's demands, its means of satisfying those demands and the national institutions long in place to cope and order them. In that one thought is the inevitability that royalty will have little place in the United Kingdom it has ruled over for close on ten centuries.

Endnote

'What is the finest sight in the world? A coronation. What do people talk about most? A coronation. What is delightful to have passed? A coronation.'

Horace Walpole, 1761

A List of Kings and Occasional Queens

English and British Monarchs

Saxon
Athelstan (924–39)
Edmund I (939–46)
Eadred (946–55)
Eadwig/Edwy (955–59)
Edgar (959–75)
Edward, the Martyr (975–78)
Aethelred II, the Unready (978–1013, unseated)
Swein Forkbeard (1013–14)
Aethelred II, the Unready (restored, 1014–16)
Edmund II (1016)
Cnut (1016–35)
Harthacanute (1035–37, unseated)
Harold, Harefoot (1037–40)
Harthacanute (restored, 1040–42)
Edward the Confessor (1042–66)
Harold II (1066)

Norman
William I (1066–87)
William II, Rufus (1087–1100)
Henry I (1100–35)
Stephen (1135–54)

Anjou
Henry II (1154–89)
Richard I, the Lionheart (1189–99)
John (1199–1216)
Henrry III (1216–72)
Edward I (1272–1307)
Edward II (1307–27)
Edward III (1327–77)
Richard II (1377–99)

Plantagenet
Henry IV (1399–1413)
Henry V (1413–22)
Henry VI (1422–61)
Edward IV (1461–83)
Edward V (1483)
Richard III (1483–85)

Tudor
Henry VII (1485–1509)
Henry VIII (1509–47)
Edward VI (1547–53)
Lady Jane Grey (1553, usurper)
Mary I, Bloody Mary (1553–58)
Elizabeth I (1558–1603)

Stuart
James I (1603–25)
Charles I (1625–49)
The Protectorate (1649–59)
Charles II (1660–85)
James II (1685–88)

Orange
William III (1689–1702) and Mary II (1689–94)

Stuart (resumed)
Anne (1702–14)

Hanover
George I (1714–27)
George II (1727–60)
George III (1760–1820)
George IV (1820–30)
William IV (1830–37)
Victoria (1837–1901)

Saxe-Coburg-Gotha
Edward VII (1901–10)

Windsor
George V (1910–36)
Edward VIII (1936)
George VI (1936–52)
Elizabeth II (1952–)

Scottish Monarchs

Alpin
Kenneth MacAlpin I (848?–58)
Donald I (858–62)
Constantine I (862–77)
Áed (877–78)
Giric (878–89)
Donald II (889–900)
Constantine II (900–43)
Malcolm I (943–54)
Indulf (954–62)
Dub (962–67)

Cullén (967–71)
Amlaíb (973–77)
Kenneth II (971–95)
Constantine III (995–97)
Kenneth III (997–1005)
Malcolm II (1005–34)

Dunkeld
Duncan I (1034–40)
Macbeth (1040–57)
Lulach (1057–58)
Malcolm III (1058–93)
Donald III (1093–97)
Edgar   (1097–1107)
Alexander I (1107–24)
David I (1124–53)
Malcolm IV (1153–65)
William I (1165–1214)
Alexander II (1214–49)
Alexander III (1249–86)

Sverre
Margaret (1286–90)

Balliol
John Balliol (1292–96)

Bruce
Robert I, the Bruce (1306–29)
David II (1329–71)

Stuart
Robert II (1371–90)
Robert III (1390–1406)
James I (1406–37)
James II (1437–60)
James III (1460–88)

James IV (1488–1513)
James V (1513–42)
Mary I (1542–67)
James VI (1567–1625)
Charles I (1625–49)
Charles II (1649–51, restored 1660–85)
James VII (1685–88)
William II (1689–1702) and Mary II (1689–94)
Anne (1702–07)

Genealogy of the Kings and Queens of England, Britain and the United Kingdom

802–1066

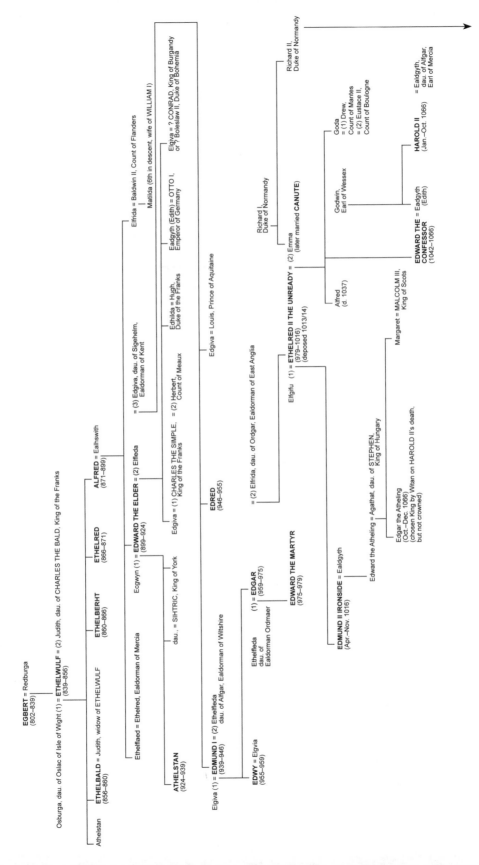

1016–1216

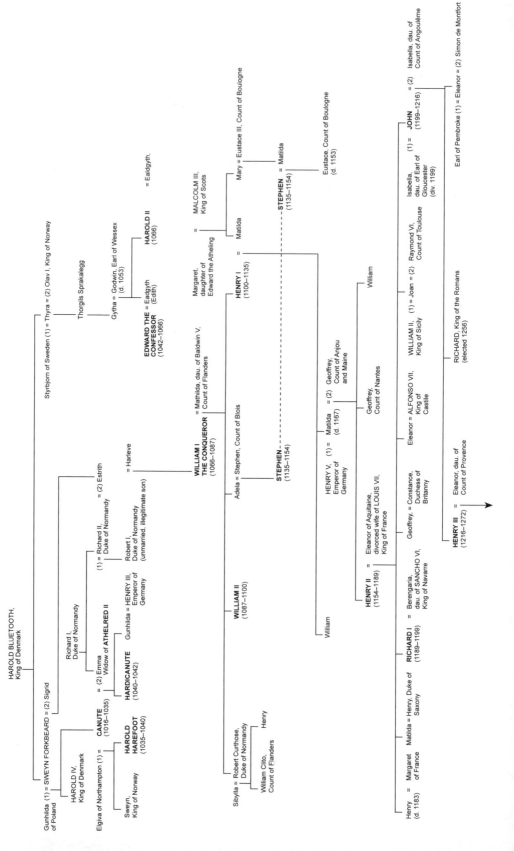

1216–1485

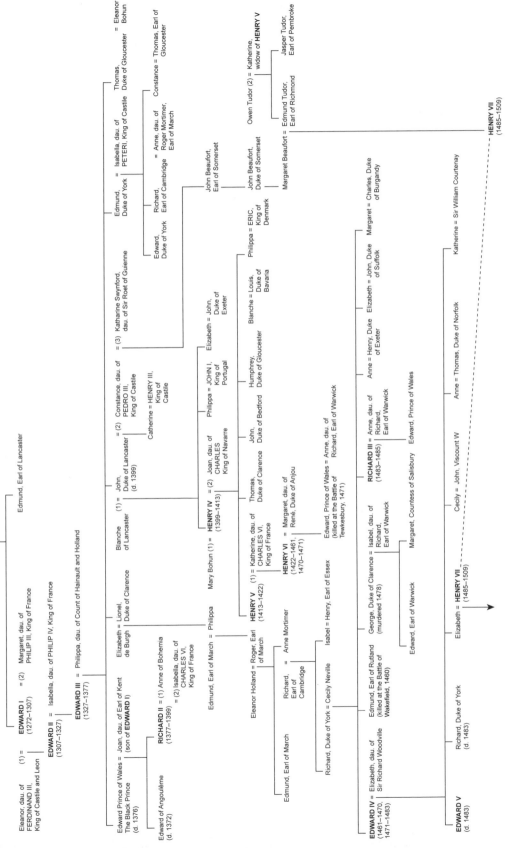

1485–1714

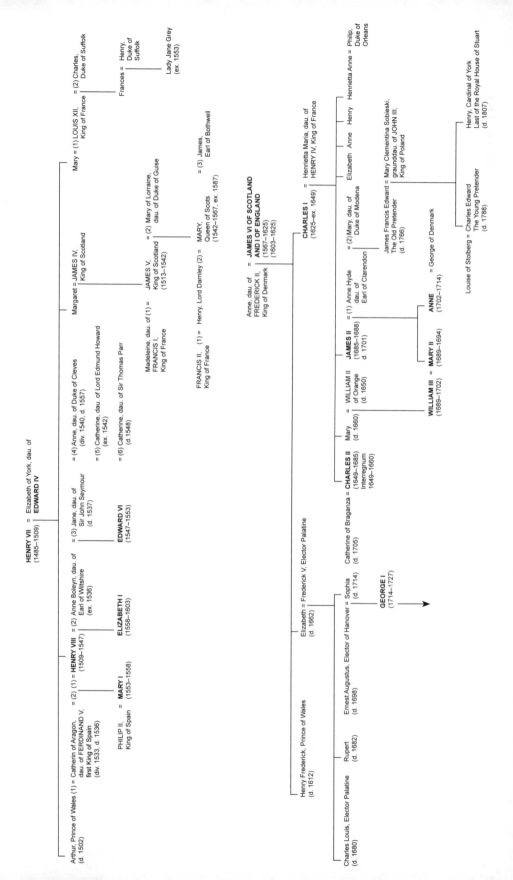

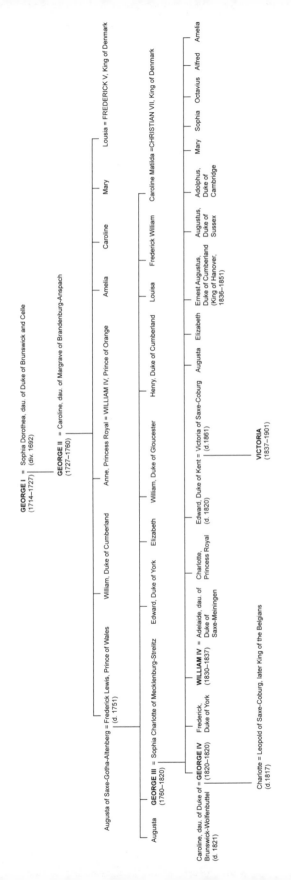

GEORGE I = Sophia Dorothea, dau. of Duke of Brunswick and Celle
(1714–1727) | (div. 1692)

GEORGE II = Caroline, dau. of Margrave of Brandenburg-Anspach
(1727–1760)

Augusta of Saxe-Gotha-Altenberg = Frederick Lewis, Prince of Wales
(d. 1751)

Augusta

GEORGE III = Sophia Charlotte of Mecklenburg-Strelitz
(1760–1820)

Caroline, dau. of Duke of = GEORGE IV
Brunswick-Wolfenbuttel   (1820–1820)
(d. 1821)

Charlotte = Leopold of Saxe-Coburg, later King of the Belgians
(d. 1817)

Frederick,
Duke of York

WILLIAM IV = Adelaide, dau. of
(1830–1837)   Duke of
              Saxe-Meiningen

Charlotte,
Princess Royal

Edward, Duke of Kent = Victoria of Saxe-Coburg
(d. 1820)   (d. 1861)

VICTORIA
(1837–1901)

Edward, Duke of York

Elizabeth

William, Duke of Gloucester

Henry, Duke of Cumberland

William, Duke of Cumberland

Anne, Princess Royal = WILLIAM IV, Prince of Orange

Amelia

Caroline

Mary

Lousia = FREDERICK V, King of Denmark

Augusta

Elizabeth

Louisa

Frederick William

Caroline Matilda = CHRISTIAN VII, King of Denmark

Ernest Augustus,
Duke of Cumberland
(King of Hanover,
1836–1851)

Augustus,
Duke of
Sussex

Adolphus,
Duke of
Cambridge

Mary

Sophia

Octavius

Alfred

Amelia

1837–present

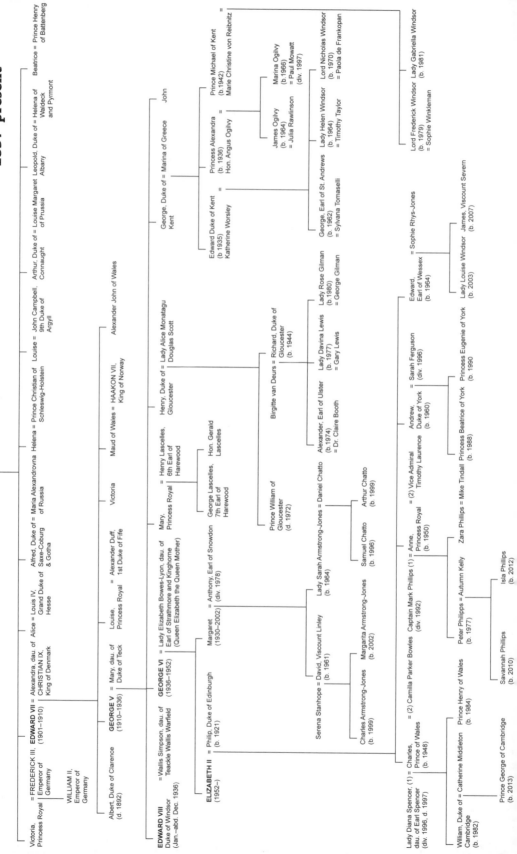

Bibliography

Bloch, Michael, *The Secret File of the Duke of Windsor*, Bantam, 1988

Bogdanor, Professor Dr Vernon, *The Monarchy and the Constitution*, Clarendon Press, 1995

Borthwick, R.L., *Long to reign over us?*, John Stuart Mill Institute, 1994

Bradley, Ian, *God Save The Queen*, Continuum, 2012

Burns, J.H., *Lordship, Kingship and Empire*, Clarendon Press, 1992

Burns, J.H.. *The True Law of Kingship: concepts of monarchy in early modern Scotland*, Clarendon Press, 1996

Cannon, John, *Modern British Monarchy*, University of Reading, 1987

Fabian, *The Future of the Monarchy*, The Fabian Commission of the Future of the Monarchy, Fabian Society, 2003

Fortescue, William, *France and 1848: the end of Monarchy*, Routledge, 2005

Fry, Michael, *The Scottish Empire*, Tuckwell Press and Birlinn, 2001

Gero, A., *The Monarchy: Heritage and Memory*, East European Monographs, 2009

Golby, John and Purdue, A.W., *King and Queens of Empire*, Tempus, 2000

Hardman, Robert, *Monarchy: The Royal Family at Work*, Ebury Press, 2012

Harrison, Ted, *Defender of the Faith*, Fount, 1996

Hitchens, Christopher, *The Monarchy*, Chatto & Windus, 1990

Jackson, Clare, *Restoration Scotland, 1660–1690*, Boydell, 2003

Kim, Yongmin, *A Comparative Study of the British Monarchy and the Japanese Emperorship*, Exeter University, 2008

Kuhn, William M, *Democratic Royalism*, Macmillan, 1996

Loughin, James, *The British Monarchy and Ireland*, CUP, 2007

Murray-Brown, Jeremy (ed), *The Monarchy and its Future*, Allen & Unwin, 1969

Olechnowicz, Andrzej, *The Monarchy and the British Nation, 1780 to the Present*, CUP, 2007

Petrie, Sir Charles, *Monarchy*, Eyre & Spottiswoode, 1933

Prochaska, F.K., *Royal Bounty: the making of a welfare monarchy*, Yale (London), 1995

Richardson, Glenn, *Renaissance Monarchy*, Arnold, 2001

Rowbottom, Anne, *Happy and Glorious*, University of Salford, 1989

Shawcross, William, *Queen Elizabeth: The Queen Mother, The Official Biography*, Macmillan, 2009

Shiell, Annette & Spearitt, Peter (Eds), *Australians and the Monarchy*, Monash University, 1993

Sinclair, David, *Two Georges: the making of the modern monarchy*, Hodder and Stoughton, 1988

Smith, Hannah, *Georgian Monarchy: politics and culture 1740–1760*, CUP, 2006

Spellman, W.M., *Monarchies: 1000–2000*, Reaktion Books, 2001

Starkey, Professor Dr David, *The Monarchy of England*, Chatto & Windus, 2004

Starkey, Professor Dr David, *Monarchy: from the Middle Ages to Modernity*, HarperPress, 2006

Storrs, Christopher, *The Resilience of the Spanish Monarchy, 1665–1700*, OUP, 2006

Strong, Roy, *Coronation, A History of Kingship and the British Monarchy*, HarperCollins, 2005

Thompson, Joe Allen and Mejia, Arthur, *The Modern British Monarchy*, St Martin's Press, 1971

Williams, Richard, *The Contentious Crown*, Ashgate, 1997

Zeigler, Philip, *King Edward VIII*, Collins, 1990

Zmora, Hillay, *Monarchy, Aristocracy and the State in Europe 1300–1800*, Routledge, 1997

Index